Are You A Food Addict?
Food Addiction Self-Diagnosis Checklist

For many, food addiction is a self-diagnosed disease. See how you score on these questions:

1. Has anyone ever told you that you have a problem with food?
2. Do you think food is a problem for you?
3. Do you eat large amounts of high calorie food in a short period of time?
4. Do you eat to overcome shyness?
5. Do you eat when you are disappointed, tense or anxious?
6. Can you stop eating without a struggle after one or two sweets?
7. Has your eating ever interfered with any part of your life?
8. Has being overweight ever affected any part of your life?
9. Do you weigh yourself once or twice (or more) a day?
10. Do you eat more than you planned to eat?
11. Have you hidden food so that you would have it just for yourself?
12. Have you felt angry when someone ate food you saved for yourself?
13. Do you worry that you can't control how much you eat?
14. Have you ever felt frantic about your size, shape or weight?
15. How many of these methods of weight loss have you tried in the past?
    — self-induced vomiting

— laxatives
— diuretics
— fasting
— compulsive exercise
— amphetamines
— cocaine
— over-the-counter diet pills, gum and caramels
— sorbitol (for laxative effect)
— chewing and spitting food
— acupuncture, acupressure
— hypnosis
— urine shots
— special food, drinks and supplements
— weight loss programs: how many? how often?

16. Have you ever felt so ashamed of the amount you eat that you hide your eating?
17. Have you been so upset about the way you eat that you wished you would die?
18. Do you overeat more than twice a week?
19. Do you invent plans in order to be alone to eat?
20. Do you seek out companions who eat the way you do?

If the answers to these questions concern you, read on.

- *Do you gain more weight than you lose after every diet?*
- *Is your yo-yo weight fluctuation getting you down?*
- *Can one cookie destroy all your good intentions?*

FOOD ADDICTION
The Body Knows
Revised and Expanded Edition

Kay Sheppard
Foreword by Father Joseph C. Martin

Health Communications, Inc.
Deerfield Beach, Florida

Kay Sheppard, LMAC, CEDS
P.O. Box 060065
Palm Bay, Florida 32906-0065

Excerpt from *Let's Eat Right to Keep Fit* by Adelle Davis, copyright 1954 by Harcourt Brace Jovanovich, Inc. and renewed 1982 by Frank Sieglinger, reprinted by permission of the publisher.
The Promises from ALCOHOLICS ANONYMOUS, pgs. 83-84, reprinted with permission.
Diagnostic Criteria for Bulimia Nervosa 307.51 reprinted with permission from the *Diagnostic and Statistical Manual of Mental Disorders, Third Edition, Revised*, Copyright 1987 American Psychiatric Association.

Library of Congress Cataloging-in-Publication Data

Sheppard, Kay
    Food addiction: the body knows/by Kay Sheppard.
        p.   cm.
    Bibliography: p.
    ISBN 0-932194-87-7
    1. Bulimia—Popular works.   I. Title.
RC552.B84S48   1989   89-15331
616.85'263—dc20   CIP

© Revised 1993, 1989 Kay Sheppard
ISBN 0-932194-87-7

Publisher: Health Communications, Inc.
             3201 S.W. 15th Street
             Deerfield Beach, Florida 33442-8190

Cover design by Andrea Perrine

Dedication

To the memory of my mother, Margaret,
to my father, Edward,
my siblings, Eileen, Bill and Peggy,
my children, John and Paul,
for your love and acceptance through all the years,
and to every Food Addict,
with love.

Acknowledgments

I wish to express my deep and lasting appreciation to these generous and gracious friends who have assisted me in the preparation of this book: Father Joseph C. Martin; Frank Webbe, Ph.D.; T. Douglas Talbott, M.D.; James R. Shaw, M.D.; Danuta Bock; Judith Coates; Dinah Fawcett; George A. Mitchell, D.O.; Gary M. Weiss, M.D.; John S. Baudhuin; Margaret Lepley; Judy Neal; Frieda Dexter; Denise Epstein; Susan Arline; LeAnn Masielo; Rosemary Rogers; Melissa Duggan and Valerie Rodgers, R.N.

Appreciation to Janet Woititz, Jamie Carraway, Nancy Porter, Janet Jowers Greeson, Fred Schneider, Margot Escott and Dr. Jim Boorstin for opportunities, support, friendship and encouragement.

Special thanks to Sandra Rossi who has provided support and encouragement since day one.

Special acknowledgment to Terence T. Gorski who developed the model for chemical dependency relapse treatment and the constructs on post-acute withdrawal and addictive thinking, then helped us apply these concepts to food addiction.

Above all, thanks to the merciful God, who leads us out of addiction.

Contents

Foreword

by Father Joseph C. Martin

On one of the early morning network shows some years ago, a young M.D. from Harvard, a nutrition specialist, was asked about the 50 diet books stacked between him and the interviewer. "Are these any good?" he was asked. "If one of them were any good," he said, "there would be no need for the other 49!" He said it all.

Kay Sheppard, in *Food Addiction: The Body Knows*, attacks the problem of food *addiction*, maintaining a position almost no others in the field hold — that some foods can be as addictive as cocaine or alcohol or any of the other substances that are accepted and acknowledged as being addictive.

Ms. Sheppard shows her grasp of the subject when she points out that obesity is a *symptom* of addiction, an external manifestation of binge eating. She does not recommend diet, a regimen geared only to drop pounds, but a lifetime plan of eating that precludes the intake of the foods one is addicted to, just as Alcoholics Anonymous precludes the intake of alcohol while allowing the use of other beverages such as water and milk.

It would be well for the compulsive eater to get proper treatment in order to discover what food one is addicted to and adopt a plan geared to a healthy regimen of food. Body chemistry differs radically from individual to individual. For example, many alcoholics find they have an instant problem with sweets after they get sober (alcohol and sugar are both composed of carbon, oxygen and hydrogen); however, this is not true of all alcoholics.

I discovered that my own intake of sweets and a few other things got out of control and the resulting increase in weight became a threat to my health and life. In June of 1987, I entered treatment at a facility for food addiction in Florida, under Ms. Sheppard, where I got a handle on my eating habits.

I feel that the sooner professionals acknowledge that foods can be as addictive as alcohol, the sooner rational ways of eating will be developed to help the compulsive eater. This book is a pioneer effort in solving eating problems. I am convinced that no other problem eater (bulimic, anorectic) can be happy either until, with help, he or she finds the answer in a treatment center that knows what addiction is about.

Read this book. It will open doors!

Preface

Consider this question, humorous though it may seem: "Can gummy bears and marshmallow chicks really be vicious killers?" As silly as that sounds, for certain individuals who are sensitive, refined carbohydrates can trigger the addictive process.

Twelve years ago when I sought to understand what food addiction was all about, I found a quotation in *Let's Eat Right To Keep Fit* by Adelle Davis: "When the blood sugar is low, the resulting irritability, nervous tension and mental depression are such that a person can easily go berserk. If hatred, bitterness and resentments are harbored, and perhaps a temporary psychological upset causes a person to go on a candy binge or makes it impossible to eat or digest food, the stage is set; violence or quarreling can occur for which there may be no forgiving. Add a few guns, gas jets or razor blades, and you have the stuff murders and suicides are made of. The American diet has become dangerous in many more ways than one." (1)

Thus she described in one paragraph the relationship between food and mood and the dilemma of my life and the life of every food addict who walks innocently into the devastating world of food and drink. Without intervention, food addiction will relentlessly rob the unsuspecting victim of all joy and happiness.

In the pages of this book, I wish to show that food addiction is a disease with symptoms and characteristics which can be recognized, that treatment is available and that with accurate information and support, people do recover. Yet currently, despite the availability of recovery programs, only a small number of food-addicted individuals get into long-term recovery. Those who continue to eat compulsively will die because untreated food addiction is always fatal. Food addiction is no less than any other addiction in terms of suffering and adverse consequences. It can be a fatal error for food addicts to minimize the serious nature of this disease. Our morgues and hospitals are filled with its victims.

Primarily, I offer the concept of physical abstinence from binge food. This has proved to be a successful approach for many recovering people. Because it is complicated and confusing for food addicts to facilitate abstinence, a plan is offered as a guide to physical recovery. For the food-addicted individual, abstinence from highly refined foods and all other mood-altering chemicals constitutes the beginning of recovery. All recovery from addiction begins with the foundation of abstinence from mood-altering chemicals. No matter what the mind might say, a food addict's body will always respond to the ingestion of highly refined carbohydrates in an addictive manner. We are just beginning to understand what the body knows.

What Is
Food Addiction?

Kathleen,* a short woman already over 200 pounds, stuffed down boxes of candy before the gastric bypass surgery she thought would solve her weight problem. Janine drank and ate all the sugary products she could lay her hands on from the time she was a toddler until food put her in a situation where she couldn't stand to be. Margot said, "I'll do anything to keep from being fat again." "Anything" included vomiting up the junk food she binged on. Maxine has dieted, fasted and binged her way to 287 pounds. She's feeling sick, tired and hopeless. Andy used to run off the effects of all the doughnuts he ate. He doesn't run anymore but he can't stop eating doughnuts — a dozen at a time! Marilyn ate so much, she feared her

---

*All names used in this book are fictitious.

stomach would burst. She tried amphetamines, laxatives
and vomiting to control her weight.

What do Kathleen and all the others have in common?
They are all addicted to starchy, sweet food. They have all
suffered from the disease of food addiction.

In the course of my work with food-addicted individuals,
I have discovered that we have developed endless lists of
ways to deal with food addiction that all failed. Acupuncture, hypnotism, groups, clubs, programs and systems are
among the methods sought to fight this disease. The sad-
dest cases are those who have been mutilated by surgery,
such as intestinal bypass, stomach staples and liposuction.
We've cried with patients and friends who have gone
through the pain, expense and ongoing discomfort created
by procedures which resulted in no permanent improve-
ment because they treat the weight problem and ignore
the addiction. Some surgery results in ongoing physical
discomfort such as poor digestion, inability to consume
bulky food, diarrhea and general feelings of poor health.

Kathleen tells about her experience with intestinal bypass surgery.

> At age 21 a physician for whom I worked asked if I would
> allow him to perform intestinal bypass surgery on me. It
> was guaranteed that I would be able to eat all I wanted and
> anything I wanted after the operation and still stay thin.
> Need you wonder at my answer? Nothing could have kept
> me from that date in the operating room. One year later I
> still weighed 190 pounds and I was not to lose any more
> weight as the result of that surgery.

Although this represented a weight loss, Kathleen
eventually began to gain again. She was 4 feet 11 inches
and maintained a weight of well over 200 pounds after
the procedure. Her doctor wouldn't look at her when he
passed her in the corridors of the hospital. We can only
presume that he was saddened by the poor results of his
efforts. She was left with the aftermath of the surgery
because she will never enjoy normal digestion again. She
continues to experience discomfort many years later.

Worse still was the bitterness she felt which led her to say, "God and I weren't on speaking terms for many years after that!"

Food Addiction Is Chronic, Progressive And Ultimately Fatal

Food addiction involves *the compulsive pursuit of a mood change by engaging repeatedly in episodes of binge eating despite adverse consequences.* A food addict is an individual who continues to use food compulsively without regard for the negative consequences. Compulsion is always present in the disease of addiction. "Despite all judgment, reason, insight or consequence, the addicted individual continues to use the substance compulsively," according to G. Douglas Talbott, M.D. (1)

Food addicts are not weak-willed or immoral nor do they have a bad habit or behavioral problem. Rather they have a metabolic, biochemical imbalance which results in the characteristic symptoms of addiction. Food addicts are obsessed with food, preoccupied with weight and appearance and they experience progressive loss of control over the amount of food they eat.

Food addiction is a chronic, progressive and ultimately fatal disease. It is chronic because the condition never goes away, progressive because the symptoms always get worse over time and fatal because those who persist in the disease will die an early death due to its complications.

There are symptoms which are present in all addictions. It is by these indicators that we are able to recognize addictive diseases. The signs of addiction are obsession, compulsion, denial, tolerance, withdrawal syndrome and craving. Food addicts exhibit all of these signs plus distorted body image.

Obsession

Preoccupation with food is demonstrated by *frequently recurring thoughts* about *buying, preparing* and *eating food.* Thoughts ordinarily come gently into the mind. Not so with thoughts of food for the food addict. Those thoughts rise powerfully to consciousness and *allow no other thoughts to enter*. No matter how hard one tries to change, ideas of food predominate. The force of desire for food is irresistible and is followed by action. It is a psychological truth that we move toward our dominant thought. Therefore, the preoccupation with getting, preparing and eating food will continually lead to binging. Progressively, these thoughts crowd out all others until the food addict's life becomes chronically food oriented.

Anticipating food is so much a part of this disease. One who is food addicted thinks with intense desire about the next bite of binge food. "Visions of sugar plums dance in their heads" in all seasons. Food controls thought.

Compulsion

Compulsion or *loss of control* is the *inability to stop eating* after one bite of binge food. The food addict may be able to stop for indeterminate periods, but despite all resolutions will binge again. The inability to control eating is a certain sign of addiction. Loss of control — that is addiction! When an individual reaches the point where he can no longer control how much or when he eats, the line has been crossed into addiction. Brief periods of abstinence from binge eating may occur because of guilt or concern about appearance, but eventually, with the best of intentions to control intake, the food addict will be off again on another binge.

When control is lost, the addict has entered the crucial phase of addiction and will never again be able to return to controlled eating of binge food. After this phase is reached, the addict will not be able to predict how much binge food will be enough.

When a food addict loses control, it is like being driven at knife point to get and eat binge foods. There is an urgency which is never satisfied. That is the paradox of this addiction — addicts eat to feel better those foods which make them feel worse. The search for that one perfect bite is never over.

Efforts to control eating fail repeatedly. An addict will try anything to lose weight, thinking that weight is the problem — exercising to the point of exhaustion, trying every new diet, fasting to the point of starvation — always believing that this time the magic way out of the pain has been discovered. Regardless of these efforts, when the addict uses binge food again, the compulsion is triggered, creating trouble with eating again. Efforts at control fail repeatedly.

In addiction, control of thoughts and behavior is lost. As addiction progresses, losses become increasingly profound. The addict's life is no longer under her own management. Her thought processes become dominated by the thinking characteristic of addiction. Food takes over. This is a very strange concept: that the course of life is directed by items from the grocery store.

The Slimness Obsession/Eating Compulsion Partnership

Thoughts of food do not reside alone in the mind of food addicts. Obsession with food creates constant eating, resulting in concern about weight gain, which increases the distraction. As the disease progresses, the fear of obesity places the addict in a no-win dilemma. The addiction condemns one to eat, acting in direct opposition to the desire to be slim and attractive. This discrepancy between the obsession with slimness and compulsive eating results in crazy ways of dealing with this problem. Lacking information about the disease of food addiction, the victim begins to seek answers wherever a person, program or system which promises a slender image can be located.

Food addicts try all the methods within their means to find the magic way out of the suffering. Over the years, efforts to control weight and eating fail repeatedly. With each new idea for weight control hopes soar, only to result in more discouragement when the regimen proves impossible to maintain. There are many people in the world ready with yet another diet, pill, calorie-counting routine, shot or concept to remedy what they believe to be a problem of weight. As with Kathleen's surgery, these methods prove to be painful, expensive and unsuccessful. Unless the system addresses the addiction, failures will be repeated — again and again.

Most addicts try highly restricted diets. There are hundreds of them printed every year for the sampling. Diets have two things in common: First, they are usually nutritionally unsound, severely limiting food choices; and second, they don't work! The nutritional deprivation of restricted diets precipitates binging, and binging sends one out looking for the next diet! It is a vicious cycle of binge and diet, diet and binge. Going *on* diets means that soon the time will come to go *off* again. Getting on and off the diet merry-go-round keeps one in an everlasting state of hope and discouragement.

Some people take the exercise approach, thinking that increased exercise will compensate for increased eating. Again, these individuals are treating the weight issue and are unaware that the disease of food addiction cannot be treated symptomatically. Weight gain is a symptom of the illness and not the primary disease. The increased amounts of food consumed by a food addict cannot be dealt with by an exercise program. It is a delusion to believe there will be enough hours in the day or enough energy to exercise adequately to compensate for the high intake of food the addiction demands.

Another pattern of weight control with serious implications is the binge-purge syndrome. Some individuals who are trapped in the compulsive use of food use purging methods. Vomiting, laxatives and diuretics allow the binge-purger to eat large amounts of food, then rid the body of that food, thus ensuring the need for more food. The starving body calls for nutrition and the mind calls for binge food. The cycle progresses, involving greater amounts of food to be ingested and purged until there is chronic involvement in the cycle.

One patient's method of weight control was fairly unique. It seems that at a very young age, she figured a way to have the taste without the weight problem. Her grandparents owned a candy store and there was a constant supply of sweets available to her. Her method was to chew and spit her food, allowing very little to be swallowed. Her foolproof method backfired though because by the time she was in her 20s, she was spending 12 hours a day chewing and spitting (ruminating). Never did she imagine how food and her fear of getting fat could take over her life, excluding career, family and friends. No one can foresee how lonely the world of addiction will be.

Denial

Denial keeps the food addict sick. Denial is the mental process by which the addicted individual concludes that he is all right. Ignorance of the disease process and *inability for self-examination* work together to keep the addict sick. Knowing nothing about food addiction and knowing no other way to live, the addict concludes that there is nothing wrong with him. This system of denial ensures the continuation of the disease process. *Food addiction is the disease that tells us we don't have a disease.* The addictive diseases have great capacity to hide from their victim. This denial must be broken before recovery can take place.

Tolerance

Tolerance is a term which describes the *body's ability to endure contact with a substance.* This term is used in addiction studies to describe the body's ability to tolerate addicting substances. Individuals with high tolerance for alcohol can "hold their liquor." For the food addict, as food intake increases, the physiological level of tolerance to binge foods increases. The body depends on the presence of refined carbohydrates and develops the need for greater quantities. As time goes on, it takes more to get the job done. Early in the progression small amounts provide the desired effect. As time passes it begins to take much more to give the food addict relief. Increased tolerance demands increased intake of binge foods. There is not enough binge food in the world to satisfy the body's demands. *One bite is too many, a thousand not enough,* for the food addict caught in the pain of addiction.

Alcoholics who drink long enough experience a condition called *reverse tolerance* whereby the body's capacity to tolerate alcohol reverses itself and will no longer accept huge quantities of the substance. The alcoholic who experiences this loss of tolerance will get as drunk on three drinks as he did on ten in earlier times. *The food addict never experiences reverse tolerance.* This disease is one of ever-increasing tolerance for binge food. The increasing demand for binge food is evidenced by individuals who survive long enough to weigh 500 or 600 pounds or purgers who binge and vomit for all their waking hours. It is not unknown in treatment programs to find individuals who have reached such a severe stage of food addiction. Usually death occurs among those in this advanced stage. Many never realize that help is available.

Withdrawal

We know that this is an addiction because when the supply of binge food is cut off, for whatever reason, the food addict experiences withdrawal symptoms. The symptoms of withdrawal may include *dizziness, chills, nausea or vomiting, food craving, severe headache, lethargy* and *poor concentration.* These may appear to be flu-like symptoms. After long periods of eating high carbohydrate foods, it will take a period of three to ten days or more to complete the acute withdrawal stage. The intensity of withdrawal differs from individual to individual. Some people are bedridden during the course of withdrawal, while others experience less severe symptoms which barely interfere with daily routine.

During the withdrawal process, the food addict is at risk of returning to the addicting substance since consumption of addicting foods will bring relief from the discomfort of withdrawal symptoms. The danger of this is that avoiding withdrawal by eating binge food keeps the food addict in the disease. Although one bite will bring better feelings, it will trigger the addiction.

I remember my mother, who was food addicted, saying that she felt dizzy and weak on her new diet but just a little sugar made her feel better. Mom was avoiding the symptoms of withdrawal. When people say, "The first three days of a diet are the hardest," they are talking about getting through the withdrawal phase.

Withdrawal symptoms are relieved by binge food but the relief is short-lived and the symptoms will recur after a brief interval. At that point the food addict again will want more binge food. This process constitutes a vicious cycle. Each time the addict relieves the discomfort with more binge food, the addiction is triggered. Binge food keeps the addict in the disease. Completing withdrawal is the way out of the disease and establishes the foundation of recovery.

The Phenomenon Of Craving

The action of trigger foods on individuals predisposed to food addiction is manifested in the form of craving which is always present in the true food addict. Craving is misunderstood by those who have never experienced it. These are the people who tell us, "Just take a little and stop," or "It's okay to eat wheat," or "Your body won't notice just a little sugar." They don't crave, so they think that we can handle these foods and stop eating whenever we choose. Nonaddicted people get all they want every time they eat. Food addicts, on the other hand, never get enough! The disease ensures that we are never satisfied with moderate amounts of food. This is what sets us apart from normal eaters. We, who are food addicted, can never safely use addictive foods at all. Our bodies will notice if we eat any amount of addictive substances.

This craving or "tissue hunger" is a physical phenomenon which occurs *after* introducing binge food into the body. When the food addict puts binge food into the system, out-of-control hunger is experienced that de-

mands more of the same. The only way for a food addict
to set up the phenomenon of craving is to introduce binge
food into the system. People say, "I was abstinent for two
years and I had cravings all of the time." Not so. If they
were physically clean, they may have been obsessed with
food, or merely desired it, but they did not crave it. The
word *craving* deals with the body only. It occurs after
introduction of trigger foods into the body. At that point,
the reaction is a craving that demands more of the same.
This kind of tissue hunger has nothing to do with the
mind, it is a physical phenomenon. The implication regarding craving is that food addicts must ensure absolute
physical abstinence from all trigger foods. When cravings
occur, it is a good idea to review all food consumed within
the past 24 hours to identify the trigger food and eliminate it. Understanding and defining our abstinence in
order to avoid craving is an ongoing process.

All food addicts have one thing in common: Once we
start eating trigger foods, we develop the craving for
more. The only relief we can find is abstinence from binge
food. If we were to take the first bite of binge food, we
would not all react in exactly the same way. But there *is*
one thing we would all do: We would all start looking for
more food. Once the craving has started, we eat more
food and more and more until we are sick and disgusted,
and still we eat on. We must be conscientious about our
abstinence or we will suffer the distress of craving. Once
craving has started we will wish to be locked in a cage
away from all binge food in order to be safe from the
disease. If we could eat trigger food without binging, we
would be out there doing it. But the truth of the matter is
that we cannot eat trigger food and predict when we will
stop eating. We cannot take the first bite of binge food
without developing the phenomenon of craving. No one
understands this like us.

Disturbed Body Image

Self-disgust is a byproduct of food addiction. Dissatis-
faction with the body and body parts is part of the process.

As we eat addictively, fear and hatred of our fat drives us crazy. It is impossible to feel self-worth when eating is out of control. There is a direct correlation between what happens to the addict physically and the level of self-esteem. The more weight that is gained, the more self-loathing we experience and then we curse ourselves for our weakness. We blame ourselves, not the disease, for this distress.

Avoidance becomes a way of life. Food addicts avoid sex and intimacy because of body shame, unwilling to expose pudgy bodies to mates and lovers. Joanie says, "I was willing to have sex with my husband, but he never saw me in the buff. I slid under the covers fully covered so he couldn't see me." Maxine gave up sex altogether, avoiding bed until her mate was asleep.

Mirrors are shunned and dreaded. Anger and frustration surface when food addicts are forced to look in a mirror to try on clothes. Joanie shares, "It was such an ordeal to conceal the bulges. Sometimes I would pick up several items of clothing to try on, believing they would flatter me. Often I was shocked to find that the selected items were a size or two too small. Choking back the anger that would come up in my throat and blinking back the tears, I would be forced to confront in that three-way mirror the image of my bulging abdomen, thighs and buttocks. Tense and sweating, I wanted to scream and break things. Instead I would fight back the feelings and find something that would fit. As I left the store, I would either snarl at someone or make a joke about finding something that would make me look 20 pounds lighter and 20 years younger."

If the three-way mirror is a reality check, the other torture test is the scale. At the moment of truth if the scale registers a loss — elation; if there is a gain — despair! Weighing is the addiction within the addiction. The scale is the ruler of the food addict's universe. That number can make or break a day. Personal identity and happiness revolve around those numbers in the little window.

Food addicts look for disguises and wear black or navy believing certain colors or tents will hide the pounds. We hide in other ways too. Because of shame and embarrassment about size and shape, we put things off until we look better. We do without new clothes, vacations and college classes. Putting life on hold until the weight or dress size is just right, we look and feel even worse because life is dull and boring.

Mickey says she avoids going to the beach with her husband where there will be pretty little things in string bikinis. She refuses to appear in public in a bathing suit the way she looks. She is sick and tired of making excuses about going to Wet and Wild when he really wants to go. Bad feelings about what she is doing have persisted for a long time. She believes she is responsible for this problem. She is feeling guilty, fat and ugly. Mickey and her husband are both hurting from the disease of food addiction. They just don't know it yet.

Do you think your body is who you are? Food addicts become so focused on weight, body size and shape that we begin to forget that we are the sum total of our body, mind and spirit.

Recognizing
The Disease

$\mathcal{A}$ careful review of the diagnostic criteria for bulimia nervosa indicates that bulimia nervosa and food addiction are the same disorder. Many believe that the term bulimia describes only the binge-purge syndrome. The criteria show that the signs and symptoms of bulimia nervosa are the same as those of food addiction and do not exclude individuals who binge and then fast, diet and/or exercise vigorously in order to prevent weight gain. In the course of their research Brewerton, Heffernan and Rosenthal noted "the similarities of the bulimic's 'food addiction' (i.e., cravings, impulsiveness, loss of control, secretiveness, stealing the desired substance and insatiability) to the substance abuser's addictive behaviors. . ." (1)

Rapid Binge/Purge

The DSM-III-R lists and describes the diagnostic criteria for bulimia nervosa referred to in this book as food addiction. All material from the DSM-III-R appears in dark print and is reprinted with permission from the *Diagnostic and Statistical Manual of Mental Disorders, Third Ed., Rev.*, Copyright 1987, American Psychiatric Association. (2) *The essential features of this disorder are: recurrent episodes of binge eating (rapid consumption of a large amount of food in a discrete period of time).*

Therefore, a binge involves eating a greater than average amount of food in a distinct period of time on a recurring basis. Formerly the DSM-III criteria designated two hours or less as the time frame for a binge. Purgers usually end binges within 20 minutes in order to avoid the effect of the digestive juices on the food so that they bring up undigested food rather than vomit. Nonpurgers do not have that kind of pressure and may continue eating until the *binge is terminated by abdominal discomfort, sleep or social interruption.* A binge may also be terminated by exhaustion of the supply of binge food. Although, *once eating has begun, additional food may be sought to continue the binge.* A binge involves the ingestion of a large amount of food.

What constitutes a "large amount of food" varies from individual to individual. It may be hundreds of calories for one individual or thousands of calories for someone else. A binge may include one bag or box of binge food or many bags and boxes. It may involve one stop on the way to dinner at a fast food store or multiple stops.

The food consumed during a binge often has a high caloric content, a sweet taste and a texture that facilitates rapid eating. Certain types of food are chosen for a binge. Patients in treatment identify foods high in sugar, starch and fat as binge foods. These foods are the drug of choice for food addicts. The food is usually eaten secretly or as inconspicuously as possible.

Inconspicuous Eating

Gloria ate M&Ms because they are chocolate and easy to eat inconspicuously. One year her students sold candy as a fund-raising project. During that time, she ate $276 worth of M&Ms from school. She remembers because she had to put that amount in the students' kitty for the candy she ate. That was for the month of February! During the same period, she tells us, she was also eating frozen yogurt with M&Ms and stopping at four to five places to get more on the way home from work.

Secret Eating

Lana's case shows how extreme secret, isolated eating can become. She didn't leave her bedroom for five consecutive months except to go to the kitchen for binge food. She suffered severe anxiety when she re-entered the world to go to treatment.

Rapid Eating

The food is usually gobbled down quite rapidly, with little chewing. Rapid eating is the hallmark of the food addict. To answer the urgent demands of the craving, food is shoved into the mouth as quickly as possible. Chewing slows the process. The appearance of this kind of behavior is an additional reason why binging is done in secret. At the table, rapid eating is a sign of food addiction as well as "working the food," that is, maintaining contact with the food by pushing, mixing or stirring it around on the plate.

Fear Of Loss Of Control

There is a feeling of lack of control over eating behavior during the eating binge. This feeling of lack of control over eating includes intense fear of being unable to discontinue eating voluntarily. When control is lost, one has crossed the line into addiction.

Purging, Fasting, Exercise

The person regularly engages in either self-induced vomiting, use of laxatives or diuretics, strict dieting or fasting or vigorous exercise in order to prevent weight gain. People with bulimia nervosa (food addiction) *invariably exhibit great concern about their weight and make repeated attempts to control it by dieting, vomiting or the use of cathartics or diuretics. Frequent weight fluctuations due to alternating binges and fasts are common. Often these people feel that their life is dominated by conflicts about eating.* All the methods used for weight control cause problems. Those who abuse laxatives and diuretics dare not stray too far from the bathroom. Diets and fasts are impossible to maintain and bring about feelings of severe deprivation. Vomiting can be extremely awkward to accomplish at times. All extreme methods used to prevent weight gain can cause serious side effects including medical and emotional problems.

Frequent Binging

Bulimics usually have a minimum average of two binge-eating episodes a week for at least three months. Certainly, most bulimics (food addicts) exceed the number of binge-eating episodes per week designated by the diagnostic criteria. Food addicts in the middle to late stages of the addiction would be more likely to binge on a daily basis.

Overconcern With Body Shape And Weight

There is persistent overconcern with body shape and weight.
As the criteria unfold, we see a picture of an individual who has lost control over the amount of food eaten and yet has tried many different things to gain control of their weight. The mind of the food addict races with obsessive thoughts of food and worry over weight gains. She is always in a panic. Nothing about her body is right. All her best efforts result in looking bad and feeling terrible about it.

Two Case Studies

The two case studies that follow show how different patterns can fit the diagnostic criteria for bulimia nervosa. The first history is that of a young woman who fits the criteria for the binge-purge syndrome.

Margot is a 28-year-old single white female whose chief complaint is, "I just can't handle food by myself anymore."

Margot states that she has had a problem with food all her life but thinks that it is only in the last several years, after she stopped drinking, that she totally lost control over food. It was then she began binging and purging. At her worst she binges and purges six times per day, visiting three to four fast food restaurants and stores. She has been doing this for over three years. She says she'll do anything to keep from being fat again.

She has had some periods of abstinence from binging and purging but she always goes back to it. Her highest adult weight is 180 pounds, the lowest is 103 pounds. She believes her ideal weight is 110 to 115 pounds.

Her favorite binge foods are sweets and flour. Her favorite binge time is at night at home. She has had three to four months of abstinence from binge food at a time but then she will start again for a couple of months. Margot purges by vomiting and denies the use of laxatives and diuretics.

She recalls that she was chubby as a child but this was considered baby fat by her family. She lost weight at age 12 but at that point started using alcohol. She continued to use alcohol until three and a half years ago. She reports getting drunk at age 12. She has a history of blackouts and morning drinking. She now has three and a half years of sobriety in Alcoholics Anonymous. She has no Narcotics Anonymous background but does have a positive drug history. She shot speed for four years "because it kept me from getting fat." She used THC, acid — essentially every drug except cocaine and heroin. When she stopped using drugs, she began drinking heavily. At her worst, for maintenance, she was drinking a fifth of gin per day.

Margot notes that she has a family history of alcoholism, including her father and her brother. Her brother also abuses other drugs. She smoked cigarettes but stopped five years ago. Her father is 66 years old, her mother 64. She has one brother and one sister. She believes that her sister is bulimic.

She has been attending meetings of Overeaters Anonymous since she was admitted into a treatment center last year for her eating disorder. She was disappointed in her treatment, which she believes was inadequate. Margot was also treated for alcoholism in a residential treatment program, followed by six months in a halfway house for women.

Margot finished high school and has had some vocational training. She has worked as a restaurant hostess for the past four years and prior to that she had many jobs. She had one serious relationship when she was 21 but her boyfriend committed suicide. She had other relationships but none were serious involvements.

Margot describes her family as being materialistic and forgiving of any challenge she put upon them to set limits for her. She acted out throughout her childhood. Her father would always rescue her but never discussed her problems with her. She describes her mother as wanting to be her friend. She is unable to describe early childhood experiences before age five. She reports that her father was abusive toward her mother. When she questioned her mother as to why she didn't leave him, her mother told her she stayed for the sake of the children.

Margot is a pretty, slightly overweight, petite woman with a ready smile and a very cheerful manner. It appears that this manner is a cover for suppressed feelings.

Margot is positive for the following diagnostic criteria for Bulimia Nervosa 307.51:

1. Has recurrent episodes of binge eating.
2. Has feelings of lack of control over eating behavior during the eating binge.
3. Uses self-induced vomiting to prevent weight gain.
4. Exceeds the minimum of two binge episodes per week for at least three months.
5. Demonstrates persistent overconcern with body shape and weight.

Maxine is a 47-year-old married white female whose chief complaint is, "I just can't handle it any longer. I'm desperate, sick, tired and fat. I hope there is a way out."

Maxine claims that food has been a problem since she was a very small child. She remembers taking food when she was small and feeling that she was doing something wrong. As the years pass she feels she has "completely lost control." With a history of dieting and fasting since she was 13 years old, she thinks she has been on "15 or more diets." Prior to admission into treatment she was considering having her stomach stapled but was afraid the surgery would be dangerous for one so fat.

She has experienced several periods of weight loss due to dieting and fasting but always regains more weight than she lost. She says, "It's a vicious battle. I've lost weight only to gain more, yet I gain weight when I'm not trying to diet, too. My weight is always increasing and it seems like it will never stop. I used to think that there would be a place where I'd stop, but I guess not. I may reach 500 pounds someday." Her top adult weight is 287 pounds and her lowest is 145 pounds. She is 5 feet 7 inches tall.

Maxine prefers sugary and starchy foods. She binges when family members are at school or work and late at night while others sleep. She has binged four to five times daily since she "went off" her last diet seven months ago. She probably eats about 18,000 calories per day. Maxine denies vomiting and the use of laxatives or diuretics for weight control.

Maxine notes that her original family members were all "big eaters — probably compulsive overeaters." Her mother and father are deceased. Both died in their fifties of heart attacks. Her siblings are all obese. Her husband and children "like to eat, too." She suspects that food is probably a pretty serious problem in her home at this time.

She finished high school and completed one year of college before she married. She has married only one time. She worked as a teacher's aide before her children were born and has not worked out of the home since that time. She describes her marriage as "dull" and owns that it has a lot to do with her obesity. She is angry at her husband for not "doing better financially." She says she loves her three children but is glad they are out of the house and on their own.

Maxine is positive for the following criteria for Bulimia Nervosa 307.51:

1. Has recurrent episodes of binge eating.

2. Feels lack of control over eating behavior during the binge.
3. Uses dieting and fasting to prevent weight gain.
4. Exceeds the minimum of two binge episodes per week for the past three months.
5. Demonstrates persistent overconcern with body shape and weight.

Self-Diagnosis Checklist

For many, food addiction is a self-diagnosed disease. See how you score on these questions:

1. Has anyone ever told you that you have a problem with food?
2. Do you think food is a problem for you?
3. Do you eat large amounts of high calorie food in a short period of time?
4. Do you eat to overcome shyness?
5. Do you eat when you are disappointed, tense or anxious?
6. Can you stop eating without a struggle after one or two sweets?
7. Has your eating ever interfered with any part of your life?
8. Has being overweight ever affected any part of your life?
9. Do you weigh yourself once or twice (or more) a day?
10. Do you eat more than you planned to eat?
11. Have you hidden food so that you would have it just for yourself?
12. Have you felt angry when someone ate food you saved for yourself?
13. Do you worry that you can't control how much you eat?
14. Have you felt frantic about your size, shape or weight?
15. How many of these methods of weight loss have you tried in the past?

— self-induced vomiting
— laxatives
— diuretics
— fasting
— compulsive exercise
— amphetamines
— cocaine
— over-the-counter diet pills, gum and caramels
— sorbitol (for laxative effect)
— chewing and spitting food
— acupuncture, acupressure
— hypnosis
— urine shots
— special food, drinks and supplements
— weight loss programs: how many? how often?
16. Have you ever felt so ashamed of the amount you eat that you hide your eating?
17. Have you been so upset about the way you eat that you wished you would die?
18. Do you overeat more than twice a week?
19. Do you invent plans in order to be alone to eat?
20. Do you seek out companions who eat the way you do?

If the answers to these questions concern you, seek out further guidance. The path to recovery involves recognition, admission and acceptance. When we recognize that something is wrong — we identify the problem — help can be found in a treatment program, private therapy or a self-help program.

See Appendix II for discussion of proposal diagnostic criteria of "Binge Eating Disorder."

The Progression Of Food Addiction

*C*he course of the disease of food addiction is a downward path with ups and downs and side trips. It doesn't always seem to be going downhill. That's what makes it so confusing. In addiction there is happy recall of the good times, accompanied by blessed forgetfulness of the bad ones. The downward path meanders. It's not always like dropping straight down an elevator shaft. But as time passes, without exception food addiction gets worse. As the condition gets worse, life becomes increasingly unmanageable due to the progressive surrender of all that is good in exchange for the substance. This progression takes place without the knowledge or permission of the victim.

Since refined carbohydrates are introduced to children at a very early age, the disease is triggered earlier in life than any other addiction. Ordinarily children do not have access to other addictive substances as young as one or two years of age. Yet very small children are offered candy, cookies, pudding, bread and other highly refined products.

Producers of baby food continue to add sugar and starches to their products. In one case, they even went so far as to market flavored sugar water for babies, masquerading as apple juice. Recent inspection of the label on a jar of infant food revealed the following ingredients in this order: water, sugar, food starch, followed by two kinds of fruit juice. That product would be dangerous for an infant predisposed to food addiction. Often the disease is triggered and the early stages initiated long before anyone might even suspect that food is a problem.

Once the disease is triggered, little food addicts will seek out a beloved relative to provide favorite foods, usually sweets. Due to the genetic predisposition to food addiction, we suspect that some of those relatives might be food addicted, too. In my case, my favorite aunt was the supplier. She could always be counted on to maintain a huge supply of binge foods. My family loved to tell the story of the time she ate her dessert before dinner so that she would be sure to have room for it.

The earliest memory of my own food addiction was at the age of five. Someone came into my kindergarten class and announced, "There will be no chocolate milk for the chocolate milk drinkers today." I was devastated and can remember to this day the feeling of my heart sinking to my feet. But good feelings returned when the announcement was made that we would have strawberry milk instead.

Early on in the addiction, food provides good warm feelings. It brings a sense of comfort and ease. In early stages addiction makes the promise that food will always work. This is the seduction: Eating feels good. Eating relieves the tensions and frustrations of daily life. The expectation is that it will continue to work! This begins the painful search for that "perfect" bite that will bring back those feelings of comfort and security.

The young food addict shows more interest in food than other children, who can take it or leave it alone. The progression of food addiction may not begin until later for some but most adults fail to recognize the symptoms in childhood which indicate that the addiction was triggered at a very early age. A careful review of past attitudes and behaviors regarding food will reveal the facts of this matter.

Early Signs — Stage One

Preoccupation With Food

Preoccupation with food is an early symptom of food addiction. Most kids spend some time peering into the refrigerator. The food-addicted child will spend an inordinate amount of time seeking, talking about and involving himself with food. Movies mean popcorn, trips to the store include ice cream cones, Easter offers baskets of marshmallow chicks and chocolate bunnies, Christmas and Thanksgiving entail huge amounts of traditional food. For food addicts, the holidays revolve around those special foods. Those in the throes of the disease are unable to assign any meaning other than eating to the activities of life.

The food addict sees life in relationship to the next opportunity to eat. Getting through the morning brings the reward of lunch, the afternoon is bearable because the afternoon snack and dinner await. Then there is evening, blessed evening, when serious eating takes place. Evenings are free time for lots of binging without interruption.

Sneaking Food

Sometimes there are guardians of the supply who are not always amenable to the uncontrolled ingestion of food. Mom and Dad may have other ideas about how to spend an evening. Besides it's embarrassing to pig out in front of others. This brings about another early symptom of food addiction: sneaking food.

There are as many ways to sneak food as there are food addicts. This is an area where food addicts are at their creative best. Delusion operates at this level of addiction. Patterns are developed such as eating by the bite, breaking off small pieces, running a finger around the edge of the cake plate while getting only the tiniest bit of frosting. These things work for little addicts because it may take only a small amount to satisfy the disease. When tolerance increases, the cake will be demolished and everyone will wonder what happened.

As a child I locked myself in the bathroom to eat marshmallows, dates, chocolate chips and other baking supplies that Mom kept on hand. I felt guilty and scared as I satisfied the demands of my disease. Lots of us eat in the bathroom or bedroom, hiding the wrappers so that family members won't know.

The feelings and behaviors associated with all addictions begin to manifest at an early age in the food-addicted child. The young addict experiences delusion, denial, dishonesty, guilt and fear. The addictive process will establish these feelings and behaviors as a way of life. Frankly it is a way of death as we eat ourselves into physical disease and emotional anguish.

Stealing Food And Money

Food addicts steal. Whether money is stolen to buy food or food is stolen, the disease has to be satisfied. Food addicts are not different from those who are hooked on other drugs. All addictions command the addict to get and ingest the addictive substance. I can remember one instance of stealing money from my mother's purse. After running to the store to buy binge food, I experienced so much guilt that I never stole money again. I *was* able to continue to take food but money was taboo. Somehow taking food from the cupboard was more acceptable than taking money from a purse. Probably I'd never been lectured about taking food from my own kitchen.

Food addicts can become frantic in the search for binge food. Are you familiar with the tradition of saving the top tier of the wedding cake for the first wedding anniversary? A patient reported taking the top tier of her sister's wedding cake to eat when she ran out of binge foods.

Some food addicts are compulsive shoplifters who report stealing food or money for food. Others shoplift expensive clothing in order to return the items for cash refunds and buy food to support their addiction. Food addicts often work in grocery stores or restaurants just to be near food that is free for the taking. One woman reported stealing small necessities in order to save her money to buy more food. These women live with shame and the sick fear of exposure and prosecution.

Discomfort In No-Food Situations

Early on, the food addict is uncomfortable in situations where there is no food. This discomfort leads to avoiding situations where food is not available or manipulating circumstances so that food will become available. I remember finding a dime on the beach of our vacation cottage and then talking my sister into rowing our row boat a long distance to the amusement park so that I could buy candy. I hope she had her own dime because I'll bet I didn't share with her.

Food addicts usually check out situations before they make a commitment to participate. Will there be refreshments at the dance? What will you be serving? May I bring something? If you're not serving, you can bet the food addict will provide something or not be there at all.

Keeping Secrets

Addicts often cover up feelings when food, eating or weight is discussed, working to keep all activities related to the addiction a secret. There is a direct relationship between the sickness and the secretiveness. When someone pointed out how much I ate or how selfish I was about food, I wished the earth would open up and swallow me.

It was so embarrassing to be a food addict. "Just leave me alone, mind your own business and I'll be just fine," I used to say. We are not all right but we have a disease which tells us we don't have a disease. It's them, not us. If they would just keep their mouths shut, we'd be just fine. We become more and more isolated from others as we hide both feelings and eating activities.

Concern About Weight

Overweight, on the other hand, may or may not be an early symptom. I have a friend who says that he was "a thin food addict for 25 years and a fat food addict for 25 years." In the early stages, exercise, activity or a high metabolic rate may compensate for the number of calories eaten, creating the illusion that the individual can eat anything he wants and maintain an average weight. This is not always the case, though. We see many children who are obese at a very early age. "Obesity affects 27% of children and 22% of adolescents, a 54% and 39% increase, respectively, in the last 15 years." (1) I remember the dread I felt every year in elementary school when the scales were brought to the classroom with the doctor. Those annual checkups were a public shaming when the announcement of everyone's weight was made.

Self-Loathing

Reviewing our stories of childhood food addiction, the picture is very sad. We see children who are condemned to eat by the addiction and condemned by the world for being greedy and fat. *Fatty, Fatty two-by-four, can't get through the bathroom door, so she did it on the floor.* A youngster hearing that chant feels pain like a knife in the heart — disgust, with no idea how to escape the pain, is the addict's lot. This is why, as the disease progresses, there is ongoing loss of self-worth. The disease is always operating on all levels of being — physical, emotional, mental and spiritual.

Gloria, aged five, doesn't want to go back to school this September because one of the kids called her a "fat pig" last year. She has decided to eat salads because she doesn't want to be called names anymore.

Eating After Others Stop

The food addict continues eating when others stop. The second (third or fourth) helping becomes a way of life. The addict sits at meals with eyes on the serving dish, hoping that the other family members will be satisfied with one serving so those extras will be his. I recall sitting on the floor by the candy dish grabbing as fast as possible to beat the others to the final pieces. There was a sense of overwhelming urgency to get as much as possible. I know now that I was feeding my disease.

On a recent business trip, I watched with sadness as an obese young man made multiple trips to the breakfast buffet to heap his plate. I couldn't help but see that he was eating large portions, which indicated that his need was greater than even a "healthy" appetite would dictate.

Summary — Stage One

Among the early signs of food addiction we look for: preoccupation with food, sneaking food, stealing food or money to buy it, discomfort in situations where there is no food available, keeping secrets, concern about weight, self-loathing and continued eating when others stop.

Delusion, denial and dishonesty develop during the early period. Without intervention, the addiction will lead to physical diseases, emotional turmoil, mental torture and spiritual bankruptcy.

Stage Two

Loss Of Control And Attempts To Control

The next phase of food addiction involves loss of control. The addict begins to lose control over the amount of food consumed and over behavior. Life becomes increasingly unmanageable. The addict is now on a downward path and, lacking information about food addiction, has no idea what is happening. It is in this stage that food addicts start to feel very uncomfortable about the use of food and weight gains.

When out-of-control eating is first noticed, the food-addicted individual usually discovers *The Weight Problem.* It's diet time. Dieting symbolizes both the food addict's struggle to deal with the symptom and her fear of the symptom of weight gain. When assessing food addiction, we look for a pattern of strict dieting or fasting. Patterns of weight loss attempts are always present in the progression of food addiction.

In the life of every food addict, the day of the diet will dawn. Whether it's the doctor, mother or friend, someone will offer a diet which worked for someone somewhere. It may be sensible, crash or just plain crazy but it will seem like the way to go.

My first diet was a calorie counter. I guess I was sick of the shame of shopping for chubby dresses. Now there's an inspired name for a line of clothing: Chubbette — Little Chub. The folks that produced those dresses knew how to face reality. They were selling clothing to chubby girls. No abstractions for them. They called an ace an ace. Mom always remarked that she "had to walk her feet off" to find clothes because those chubby dresses weren't easy to find. So the day came when Mom was going on another diet and I chose to put the fat clothes behind me and join her.

The diet became a challenge-diet for me. I added up those daily totals of calories and strove for less than 800 per day. What elation if I came in under 800. This was very poor nutrition for a 15-year-old girl. Of course, the weight fell off and I felt thin for the first time in many years.

When the food addict becomes concerned about weight, the world will be ready to offer solutions to that problem. Characteristically, the food addict is concerned about weight, obsessed with food and has lost control over the amount of food being eaten. When efforts to control eating fail, every addict will continue to seek out new means of dealing with weight gains. When doctors offer drugs, they are accepted in innocence with the belief that the problem is weight. Who would suspect that the food itself is the problem?

For many years food addicts had access to diet pills which created problems of addiction. Those drugs are still available on the streets. Cocaine is a seductive drug which will work for weight control. Someone once said that using cocaine to control weight is like using a steam shovel to dig up a daffodil bulb. The food addict who uses drugs to deal with weight will become addicted to them.

"Some people with this disorder are subject to psychoactive substance abuse or dependence, most frequently involving sedatives, amphetamines, cocaine or alcohol." (2) For years, when I felt like eating, I smoked a cigarette. That was another addiction in action. It changed my metabolic rate and helped to keep weight down. Many food addicts who smoke continue in that addiction due to an overwhelming fear of weight gain.

Each time we try a new idea for weight control, we believe we have found the magic way out. The idea that we are addicted to specific foods eludes us. We try each new cure until the cure itself becomes an added problem.

Fasting is a tempting idea for food addicts. It seems simpler to eat no food than trying to deal with foods which cannot be controlled. There are many variations of fasting which have been conceived by the desperate, such as not eating all day until dinner time, abstaining from all food for three days and returning to the usual style of eating on the fourth day, long periods of fasting (sometimes in hospitals) followed by the slow introduction of specific foods, abstaining from all solid food and drinking only water, abstaining from all solid food and drinking whatever you like, and so on. The problem with these plans is that the body will rebel and demand nutrients and fiber. The body pleads for nutrition and the mind says BINGE. Fasting sets up the next binge. When trigger food is reintroduced, the binge cycle will start all over again.

Exercise is a common way that the food addict deals with weight. On the surface, exercise appears to be a healthy option for the overweight person. Yet exercise is another regimen which deals only with the symptom of weight gain and not the disease. Many individuals work out in order to eat more. Some become so obsessed with exercise that the time devoted to eating and exercising becomes overwhelming. Certain food addicts suffer panic attacks when their exercise time is limited by outside forces. Binging and exercising become a way of life.

Purging may seem like the magic way out of the food addiction dilemma. Laxatives, diuretics and vomiting are the usual ways for binge-purgers to rid their bodies of the enormous amounts of food consumed during a binge. The medical and emotional price is high for the practitioners of this approach to weight control. It is not unusual to practice a combination of many approaches to weight loss.

Self-Deception And The Deception Of Others

As food addiction progresses, sneaking food intensifies, leading to the deception of self and others. Here are some of the deceptive practices of food addiction:

- Buying food for others and eating it all
- Eating bits and pieces without ever acknowledging how much has actually been eaten
- Hiding food in dresser drawers, sewing machines and other unusual places
- Eating secretly
- Never counting calories when overeating
- Always counting calories when dieting and talking about it — a lot
- Purchasing small amounts of food and making frequent trips to the store
- Using artificial sweeteners in coffee and having two pieces of pie with the coffee
- Eating tiny amounts at a party and binging later at home
- Eating in the car, bedroom, bathroom, garage, backyard (even when there is no picnic)
- Hiding wrappers

- Always using the kitchen phone (being where the food is)
- Tasting while cooking
- Eating all the leftovers while cleaning up
- Never wasting any food (remember the starving children)
- Arranging to be home alone in order to binge
- Carving out the other end of the gallon of ice cream
- Making extra batches while everyone is away
- Eating huge high-calorie meals and never eating between meals
- Visiting those neighbors who bake the most
- Hanging out with other overeaters
- Taking food from friends' cupboards and candy dishes
- Freezing baked goods as insurance against eating them, then eating them frozen
- Blaming the missing sweets on the kids
- Eating the kids' Halloween, Easter and Christmas candy
- Stocking up for the holidays with ten times more food than the family needs
- Baking 44 varieties of Christmas cookies for gifts

Thus addicts are able to hide the amount eaten from friends, family — and certainly from themselves — while ensuring an adequate supply of food to satisfy the increasing need for more.

Making Excuses

Endless excuses are made for the mountains of food consumed in food addiction. Overeating is blamed on boredom, nervousness, family problems, medical problems and the old standby, *I needed a pick-me-up.* We say things like, *You'd eat too if you had (a job, kids, husband, schedule, mother, father, sister, brother, teacher) like mine!* The excuses made for overeating are really an attempt to make sense out of an eating pattern which makes no sense at all. Then there are the excuses made for weight gains: *It must be my metabolism — or my glands — or I'm holding water.* The truth of the matter is that life is becoming increasingly more unmanageable. We mistakenly believe that our problems are causing the eating, not knowing that the addiction is causing our problems.

Lethargy, Irritability And Depression

During this second stage of addiction, increased sensitivity to carbohydrates results in increased irritability, tiredness and depression. It becomes difficult to get out of bed in the morning. Every act of daily life requires more energy than can be summoned. Family relationships become strained. Increased weight and lethargy cause lowered feelings and those close to the food-addicted individual share the pain.

The Final Stages

Efforts To Control Binging Fail Repeatedly

Efforts to control eating fail during the late stage of addiction. I had attended a well-known weight loss program several times. The program appeared to work well for me and I achieved a substantial weight loss. But before I could start the maintenance program, I had slipped back into the old pattern of eating excessive amounts of refined carbohydrates. I recall my husband asking, "What happened to your diet?" It was painful to admit, "It went out the window." That admission resulted in guilty feelings because of the huge amount of money I had spent on the program plus the cost of special food. I remember that I didn't want to talk about it. I was too embarrassed. Time and time again, we desperately try to find ways to deal with the weight, never realizing that the problem is not the weight but the addiction itself.

Promises and resolutions fail, whether they are made to self or others. I was destined to fail on a weight loss program which provided daily amounts of my addictive substances of refined carbohydrates. Without accurate information about addiction, we don't even look for a method of recovery other than a weight loss regimen.

We are destined to fail and suffer another blow to self-worth each time we fail to lose or maintain the loss of weight. Guilt and remorse become a way of life as we spend money, which could have been used better for our family, on every crazy new promise of thinness. For instance, I once went on a no-carbohydrate diet which lasted less than a day. It ended in binging on scallions because I was craving carbohydrates. A friend suggested her fast to me, which allowed you to drink anything you wanted for three days and then go on any diet you wanted. I wanted to drink milkshakes but never got to the diet. All of these attempts ended ultimately in more weight, not less.

Loss Of Interest In Family, Friends, Other Pursuits

Eventually, we lose interest in other things, as shopping, cooking, baking, dining in and dining out become our main sources of pleasure. We become so food oriented that most of our activities have to do with eating. In my own case I became a stodgy homemaker — no bright promises in my life. I was dull, fat and tired and had no aspirations for more than that.

Food addiction breeds in isolation. We plan ways to be alone so that we can eat alone. Eating alone brings its own unique kind of comfort. Often interesting manipulations are needed to ensure being alone with our food supply. We have to manufacture activities for the family so that they will be away while we binge at home. Mary couldn't wait for her husband to go out the door, so she could grab her sweets. Or we may invent ways to be off in the car by ourselves, where we can eat without comments from other family members. I used to fear having a fatal accident caused by hands sticking to the steering wheel, rendering me incapable of operating the car. When it comes to eating alone, Lana gets the prize! For five months, she left her room only to go to the kitchen for binge food.

Work And Family Problems

It's not surprising that this stage of food addiction is characterized by marked self-pity and negative thinking, as well as work and family problems. Serious consequences such as divorce and separation begin at this stage of the addiction. There is radical deterioration of relationships. At this point many reach out for help either to the medical profession for the many physical ailments suffered or to the mental health specialist due to emotional symptoms. Often professionals fail to recognize food addiction and they treat the symptoms rather than the disease. This further frustrates the addict who attempts to cooperate in treatment and yet receives no benefit from that treatment because the addiction has not been addressed.

Eileen, who had been in therapy prior to food addiction treatment, asked me, "Did I have a chance to resolve my therapy issues while I was a practicing food addict?" I said, "No." She replied, "I didn't think so. In fact, right now I can't remember any of those old issues." Eileen was one of the lucky ones. Her counselor learned to recognize food addiction. We can't expect positive results from treatment if clients are walking around drunk on binge food.

Life is falling apart for the food addict in the late stages of this chronic disease of food addiction. The addict hopes that major changes will affect life for the better; a new home, new spouse, new town or new job holds promise that life will be better. But the old adage that we take ourselves with us holds true. Nothing gets better. The spiral is ever downward. Everything is worse because food has taken over and we don't even understand this cause of turmoil in our lives. We blame those about us for our misery and they blame us, while none of us recognizes that our addiction to food has kept us in a state of altered mood. We have lost control over the amount we eat, what we eat and how we behave. We are totally obsessed with eating, weight and dieting.

Emotional, Physical, Moral And Mental Deterioration

At this stage of the progression, we are deteriorating on all levels — emotional, physical, mental and moral. Anger, irritation and resentments are with us all the time. Blame leads to unreasonable resentments against those who still remain in our lives causing radical deterioration of family relationships. We begin to avoid family members.

Maxine recalls staying up late at night and sleeping late in the morning to avoid her husband as much as possible. Lonely late-night hours provide time to binge privately. This is the lonely disease demanding that we stay separated from those we might love.

Declining physical health, self-image, relationships and mood are typical of this stage of the disease. There are often chronic disturbances of mood involving depression, low energy and fatigue, low self-esteem, poor concentration, anxiety, difficulty making decisions and feelings of hopelessness. Some patients report chronic feelings of emptiness. The declining emotional condition coupled with recurring medical crises create a burden which is almost too much to bear. Suicidal thoughts and acts as well as other self-mutilating behaviors are reported.

Neglect Of Good Nutrition

There is now an urgent need for larger amounts of food and it no longer matters what we eat. Stale crackers and fancy desserts will both answer the body's demand for refined carbohydrates. Rapid weight gain is a consequence of this indiscriminate eating. Panic sets in when we discover that we are no longer able to stay on any diet for any period of time. The truth of addiction plays itself out in our lives. There is no sane way to manage an addiction, no way to manage addiction at all. There is only self-deception, gradual loss of hope and pain. Purgers suffer their own hell when each day becomes a constant round of binging and purging. From kitchen to bathroom, it is a vicious cycle of stuffing food, vomiting and diarrhea that results in a sore body and a sore heart.

None of our old solutions works and we feel hopeless, helpless and full of remorse.

Food Is The Main Source Of Security

At this point in the progress of the disease, food is our main frame of reference. All our living experiences are translated into food terms. When we are thirsty, we eat juicy fruits or drink sugary drinks. We feed our addiction when normal folks might drink water. When we are hot, we eat cold foods; when cold, we eat hot foods. Even sickness provides an excuse to eat. Food addicts treat illnesses with food. All physical and emotional sensations translate to ingesting food. The one sensation which we usually do not have to deal with is normal hunger except when we are in the dieting mode. When we do feel hungry, we usually also feel panic or anxiety. Food has become our principal source of security. It has replaced God.

Panic: Obsession And Compulsion Take Over

We are so obsessed with food that it is like being driven at knife point to get and eat our addictive substance. We are allowed no rest. We must make constant trips to get and eat our binge foods. Why do we do it? *We can't not do it.* We are caught up in the path of a relentless tornado and we react with terror because we know of no salvation. Binging fills every waking hour.

Complete Defeat

We give up and go insane, die or recover. Those are the only ways out. Those who know of no solution surrender to the disease and continue to eat insanely. Those who never find recovery surrender to the disease and die an early death, sometimes by suicide. Many continue in the denial and delusion of the disease, hoping for an easy way out. A fortunate few surrender, to live an abstinent life in recovery. My own mother surrendered to the disease when she said, "Kay, I've given up. For the rest of my life, I'm going to eat the way I want to." She just couldn't fight it any more. She died an early death because we couldn't figure any way out of the disease for her. Some of us are luckier — we find recovery.

The Primitive Brain – Seat Of Addiction

$\mathcal{M}$ost of the human population who eat highly refined foods are not subject to food addiction. They have not inherited the genetic predisposition to addiction. However, there are large numbers of people who are genetically susceptible to addictions. They have inherited the brain chemistry peculiar to food addicts. Often from earliest infancy these individuals react differently to refined carbohydrates when they ingest them because they have a biogenetic disease, that is, they have a biological defect handed down from generation to generation.

All addiction involves the compulsive pursuit of a mood change by engaging repeatedly in a process despite adverse consequences. An addict is an individual who continues to use a substance compulsively, such as food, alcohol or drugs without regard for the negative consequences. Compulsion is always present in the disease of addiction.

"Despite all judgment, reason, insight or consequence, the addicted individual continues to use the substance or practice the behavior compulsively," according to Dr. Doug Talbott in his address to the International Association of Eating Disorders Professionals in Atlanta, Georgia. (1) Despite the irrational nature of the process, the addicted individual will continue to pursue alteration of reality. "These individuals are not bad, dumb, weak, evil or crazy — they have a biogenetic disease," Dr. Talbott says. (2) "The answer to this compulsive path of self-destruction lies within the brain itself." (3) Addiction has a biological basis related to the way the brain uses its neurotransmitters. These transmitters effect a change of balance within the brain which brings about an improved feeling.

Hypothalamus, Seat Of Instinctual Feelings

The specific area of the brain with which addiction is associated is the hypothalamus. All humans have two separate brains, the new brain and the old brain. The new brain or cortex is the area of thoughts, decision making and evaluation. The old brain, of which the hypothalamus is a major part, is the seat of instinctual feelings.

Man, as an individual and as a species, has survived and evolved due to the fact that buried deep within his physical brain, there is an ancient instinctual survival brain which governs the functions of aggression (fight), escape (flight), reproduction, thirst and hunger. This old brain, located within the hypothalamus, is the seat of the primitive, instinctual feelings of hunger, anger, thirst, sex drive and fear. These have been identified as the foundation of all human needs upon which existence depends. The hypothalamus works by sending messages to the new brain (cortex), where decisions are made as to what to do about human needs. Under ideal circumstances, the old brain sends a message to the new brain with a specific request, the new brain determines what to do and at that point a specific response satisfies a specific request. For instance, when a cave man needed food, he sought to satisfy his hunger by hunting, gathering and eating. He satisfied his thirst at a stream or pool. Like all members of the animal kingdom, the cave man enacted basic survival behavior.

Hypothalamus → message → cortex → appropriate response

A healthy response looks like this:

Identified need → thirst → decision → drink water

Had the cave man ignored the messages sent out from the survival brain, death would have resulted. He would not have fulfilled his survival needs in such a way as to continue life, satisfy his appetite and promote feelings of well-being. Had this been the case, our species would have ceased to exist.

What happens when the brain's chemistry malfunctions? How does the message get so confused that all of the body's needs are met with an addictive substance? Why is it that most people get up in the morning and eat to live, while food addicts get up and eat to die? We suspect that in addiction there is an aberration of the system, a short circuit in the neurotransmitter messenger service. In addiction, the specific request is sent but the message gets garbled so that in the later stages of addiction one response takes care of everything. There is no longer any need to make a decision. The addictive substance will answer every need because it will restore balance within the survival brain.

The addictive response looks like this:

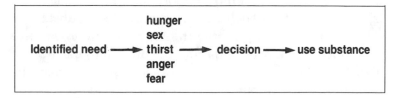

When an addict says, "I ate over it" or "I drank because of it," it's not because he's bad, dumb, crazy, weak or evil, but because the message got mixed up in his brain. The old brain, which was designed to ensure survival by sending out messages to the new brain, is impacted by drugs, food, sex and exercise. When the body signals the brain that a need exists, the brain responds by releasing chemical signals which cause an action to fill the need, as described. Two chemical messengers the brain normally produces are called endorphins and enkephalins. These two chemicals seek out and attach to mating receptors in the brain. The receptors accept only those chemicals whose molecules have the right shape. It is like a key fitting into a lock. (4)

Effect Of The Endorphin — Enkephalin Metabolism On The Brain

It has been theorized that in addiction there is an abnormality of the endorphin-enkephalin metabolism within the old survival brain. Whatever substance or behavior changes the neurotransmitters, thereby producing abnormal metabolism of the neurotransmitter system within the old brain, results in addiction.

The enkephalins seem to influence such basic processes as pain transmission, respiration, motor activity, endocrine control and limbic functions involving the emotions. It is possible that the production of enkephalins and endorphins, the brain's natural pain-relieving and pleasure-causing neurotransmitters, is abnormally low because of either decreased production or rapid destruction in addicted individuals. When the endorphins are low, the brain is on edge, making such people susceptible to substances which will artificially soothe the brain and improve feelings. Such substances will bring the brain into balance. In addiction, the use of certain substances starts a chain of bodily events. Although that chain of events differs for each substance, all of them result in the production of brain chemicals which produce an improved feeling. That improved feeling is the object of addiction.

"Most clinicians and researchers now embrace a multidetermined model of pathogenesis of bulimia nervosa that includes biological factors which may predispose to, perpetuate or exacerbate the disorder. There has also been over the past 10 years a great increase in knowledge regarding the neurotransmitters involved in the complex central and peripheral regulation of appetite behavior: serotonin, dopamine, norepinephrine, endogenous opoids and gastrointestinal hormones, such as cholecystokinin, have all been found to play a role in the control of food intake. Finally, these substances continue to be implicated in other psychiatric disorders that have either phenomenological or familial overlap with bulimia nervosa." (5)

Serotonin, The Calming Chemical

High carbohydrate food facilitates the release of serotonin. According to nutrition researcher Judith J. Wurtman, Ph.D., from the Massachusetts Institute of Technology, "Serotonin is the calming chemical. When the brain is using it, feelings of stress and tension are eased." (6)

"When carbohydrates are digested, the pancreas releases insulin. In addition to regulating blood sugar, insulin decreases the bloodstream concentration of amino acids — except for tryptophan. Higher tryptophan levels then reach the brain and the brain uses them to manufacture a chemical called serotonin." (7) In fact, it seems that carbohydrate food is the most effective precursor of serotonin. According to Brewerton et al, "Behavioral and clinical studies in animals and humans suggest that altered function of the neurotransmitter serotonin may be of major significance in mediating the prominent clinical symptoms in bulimia." These researchers go on to say, "The appetite, affective and impulsive features of bulimia have all been associated with possible alterations in serotonin transmission." (8) The calm feeling which is produced plays a role in food addiction.

"Taking sugar or some substitute for sugar is one way a person suffering from this disturbance — an addictive person — can temporarily quiet his or her physiological hunger and feel 'normal' or 'relaxed' for a while, however briefly." (9) It's no wonder that the food addict's diet increasingly includes more and more carbohydrates. "Carbohydrate-rich, protein-poor meals increase the synthesis and release of brain serotonin." (10)

Physical dependence is the essence of food addiction, a disease which interferes with the individual's ability to function normally. This diseased state is not a conscious choice made by the addict. No one sits in first grade and plans to be a food addict.

The Addict: A Powerless Vehicle For The Addictive Substance

When the brain's survival mechanism goes awry, it results in an addiction which operates at the most elemental level. Addiction impacts on the survival brain with fatal results. An addict *does not decide* to use chemicals, he is *compelled* to do so. His brain and body chemistry operate in an addictive manner in the presence of addictive substances. He cannot think or act his way out of it without support and accurate information. Therefore, he acts in a self-destructive manner. His survival brain can no longer ensure his survival. Instead, his brain chemistry works to ensure his destruction. Addiction is a survival issue because the survival message has gone awry. It is so turned around that the brain facilitates that which will kill, using the survival mechanism to ensure death.

People talk about addictions as though addicts consciously choose addiction. The disease influences choices based on the substances that have been introduced into the system. Addiction operates automatically at the physiological level, no matter how hard the fight to resist. Delusion and denial are automatic. The addict is a vehicle for the addictive substance. That's what *powerless* means.

Recovery: Dealing With Scrambled Messages

Recovery, on the other hand, operates at the cognitive level of the brain. The addict must use his new brain to deal with the failure of the messenger service within the old brain. There are two things the addict must understand in order to recover:

1. Every time an addict ingests an addictive substance, the disease will be triggered at the physiological level.
2. During the course of the addiction the conscious mind has been operating in a deluded manner.

Addicts can't trust their minds or bodies because both are in the grasp of the disease. Since addiction operates at the survival level, the recovering individual must have accurate information, strong support and guidance to see him through the withdrawal and early recovery process. Since the thought processes have been affected by the addiction, newcomers to recovery must rely on older members literally to do their thinking for them. Newcomers to recovery cannot trust their logic. It is never possible for an addict to think his way out of addiction. No matter how great the intellect, it can never be used to change the fact that the addiction is relentlessly operating at the physiological level.

Early recovery is a convalescence period used for fundamental healing, stabilization and withdrawal from the addictive substance. Recovering food addicts must take care of their basic human needs.

Marcie phoned because she is feeling out of sorts: She missed a meal, missed her recovery program meeting, failed to get proper rest and just feels miserable. Marcie's recovery needs are not being met. Dr. Talbott reminds us of *HALT*, "Don't get too *H*ungry, *A*ngry, *L*onely, *T*ired." (11) In other words, recovering food addicts cannot afford to abuse themselves.

In the recovery process when we feel an urge, we must figure out what the real need is and answer that need with nutrients, good counsel or rest. Using binge food to deal with feelings is no longer an option. We must begin to address our real feelings and problems in a constructive way. In recovery, we use our thought processes (new brains) to learn the tools to keep our old brains in check. Eating over a problem is the last thing a food addict can afford to do!

5

The Addictive Foods

What are the problem substances? Since food addicts do not overeat all foods, see if you can identify the addictive ones now described.

Marilyn describes her carbohydrate sensitivity, then makes the connection between her food binges and her unhappiness:

> At the age of four or five I would get angry when someone (usually my sister) would get to eat lots of snacks, like extra chocolate in milk or extra ice cream. I would cry and hold my breath until I fell down. I became obsessed with ice cream. I couldn't get enough. I always wanted to lick the bowl of cake or cookie batter.
>
> When I began smoking pot in junior high school, food became much more magical. I ate everything from sugar cinnamon toast to whatever there was for dinner. I ate huge

amounts of macaroni and casseroles. I recall getting high with girlfriends and baking cakes. This became a weekend ritual.

I knew I was eating too much and I kept telling myself I'd quit binging. I made many promises to myself that I'd stay out of the refrigerator and the cupboards but my good behavior never lasted. I kept promising my boyfriend I would lose weight and quit binging. I ate more than he did.

The pattern of my addiction to food changed through the years. I consumed large amounts of sweet foods — two or three large pieces of cake at a time when I was younger, many huge pieces as I got older. I ate huge bowls of ice cream. A lot of the time I didn't get enough because then I would have got into trouble with my mom. I got lots of cookies, cupcakes and sweet breads because my grandmother did quite a bit of baking. I always got to lick the beaters, the bowls and the spoon. That seemed like a reward. To keep from getting in trouble for eating the rest of the cake or the rest of the ice cream, I started finding ways of stealing.

During grade school I stole candy bars and gum from the local store along with the rest of the kids. Then I stole money from my grandmother just so I could have extra snacks at school and get ice cream after school. If I didn't have any money and there wasn't much food around during my pot-smoking period, I would smoke so much I passed out.

My major binge food later in life when I was craving sugar was cookie batter — my version. I would cream together butter and sugar, add eggs, flour and vanilla extract with no intention whatsoever of baking cookies. When I actually did make cookies, I would wonder why the recipe never yielded what it said it would. If there was a box of cake mix around, I could eat it straight from the box. No added ingredients necessary!

I ate so much that my stomach actually felt as though it was going to burst. I would get very bloated, get headaches whenever I stopped eating sugar, which would prompt me to eat more sugar. I was very tired and never wanted to do homework because I ate so much after school. Later as I became more worried about my weight, I began taking amphetamines to control my binging during the week. I still ate lots during the weekends. Then came two years of laxative abuse, then vomiting to control weight. I was always worried about my complexion, having always had a problem with it

due to the kinds of food I ate — chocolate and sweets. It was
an ongoing problem and still is.

This way of life affected my emotions. I thought I was
doing it to make myself feel better but it actually caused a lot
of anxiety and insecurity about my looks. Then I would
strive to be even better and when I couldn't be, I fell deeper
into self-pity.

I was a habitual liar and a "people-pleaser." I could put on a
happy face when I didn't feel happy if I thought it would get
me something. Otherwise I didn't care and would just be a
grouch. When I was with my mother, I was as nasty as I could
be. I would get very temperamental after binging and I'd
scream at my mother, being very vicious to her at times. Now
I just get very bitchy and unbearable to be around. I attempted
suicide when I was 15. I would often (and still do) hate myself
after a binge. I feel so disgusted and I continue to take it out
on the people around me — very brutally in fact. My mother
was the main target of this emotional outlet for me. After
Mom died, I abused my boyfriend and my roommate.

I'm sure things would be much different financially for me
if not for my compulsive eating. I could have saved a lot of
money had I not bought all that binge food. I would have
been a much more productive person had I not been drugged
out on food so much.

Highly Refined Carbohydrates

**Food addicts typically overeat highly refined carbohy-
drate foods; those foods which are quickly converted to
sugar.** Sugar and starch-based foods appear to be so
innocent! You might wonder how such innocent-appear-
ing foods could show up in the story of addiction. Take a
look at the part the refinement process plays in the
addictive process.

Every addictive substance has been through the refinement process. All addictive substances start as something
natural. "After all, heroin is nothing but a chemical. They
take the juice of the poppy and they refine it into opium
and then they refine it to morphine and finally to heroin.
Sugar is nothing but a chemical. They take the juice of the
cane or beet and they refine it to molasses and then they

refine it to brown sugar and finally to strange white crystals." (1)

How are problem foods identified? We could examine endless lists of various binge food. In this way food plans could be individualized for every food addict. The danger of that approach is that errors would be made which would make it impossible to get out of the addiction.

Refined carbohydrates "stimulate increased transmission of dopamine, serotonin and norepinephrine. As the synapses become flooded with these neurotransmitters, a feeling of euphoria results and craving for more refined carbohydrates is stimulated." (2)

"One actually becomes intoxicated by the sugar, white flour and other refined carbohydrates as they act as alcohol in the blood system and hypothalamus." (3)

According to Richard J. Wurtman, M.D., Director of the Clinical Research Center at M.I.T., "We observe that a sizable portion of obese subjects seeking assistance in weight reduction consume as much as half of their total daily intake as carbohydrate-rich snacks and that this behavior is often associated with strong feelings of carbohydrate craving. Conceivably this appetite disorder reflects an abnormality in the process that couples carbohydrate consumption to the release of brain serotonin. Many patients describe themselves as feeling anxious, tense or depressed before consuming the carbohydrate snack and peaceful or relaxed afterwards. It may be more than a coincidence that dietary carbohydrates and both major classes of antidepressant drugs, the monoamine-oxidase inhibitors and the tricyclic-uptake blockers, are thought to increase the quantities of serotonin present within brain synapses. Perhaps the subjects snacking on carbohydrates are unknowingly self-medicating." (4) This is a clear indication that *the body knows!*

If I binge on sugar in one form, I will binge on sugar in all forms. And the same is true for all the foods of addiction. The addiction mechanism cannot differentiate one refined carbohydrate from another. "Digestion begins in the mouth as starches are changed to disaccharides or

double sugars." (5) Refined carbohydrates will always
trigger the addiction in carbohydrate sensitive individuals.
This is not a matter of likes and dislikes. Instead, it is a
situation which requires identification of all foods that
will trigger the addiction at the physiological level. "Perhaps less emphasis should be placed on the sugar versus
starch dichotomy and more attention should be directed
to the influence of rapidly absorbed versus slowly absorbed carbohydrate foods on human adiposity." (6)

Addiction is such a serious condition that we dare not
trust guesswork in the identification of addictive foods.
I've heard people say, "I'd never binge on that food because
I don't like it!" The important question is, like it or not,
will it trigger the addiction? Remember, the body knows!
If I trigger the addiction with a food I'm not fond of, I'll
quickly go to food that appeals to me and wonder what
happened. Why am I at it again? Remember, the body will
always act in an addictive manner. So why bother with
foods you don't like if they offer a threat to recovery?
Think about it! Could denial be at work here? Remember,
a food addict cannot think or act his way out of addiction.

Recently a young woman shared that she had relapsed.
She traced the trigger food back to the gravy she had
decided to eat. At the time she ate it, she thought, "Just
that little bit of flour won't bother me." The fantasy was,
"My body won't notice that I just ate an addictive substance." Such rationalizations will not change the course
of addiction because *the body knows* otherwise.

People worry that if given a generic food plan which
eliminates all refined carbohydrates they will be deprived
of a favored food which may be safe for them. The
greater worry is that we won't discover and eliminate all
foods of addiction. The fact is that we cannot recover
until we identify, withdraw from and abstain from all
addictive foods.

Twelve years ago, when I began recovering from food
addiction, I was given a very low-carbohydrate food plan. It
was so low in carbohydrates, it didn't even allow green
peas. My doctor called it The Cave Man's Diet. The good

news was that it was an *abstinent* food plan. It worked because it eliminated *all* my binge foods. The bad news was that it eliminated many foods that I could have tolerated. Basically, it was a restricted diet that eliminated whole groups of foods such as grain and starchy vegetables. People on that diet were nutritionally deprived.

For me The Cave Man's Diet resulted in a spectacular change in mood. In the first few weeks, I started to feel better than I had felt in years. What a miracle that seemed to be — to move from lethargy and depression to a mood of elation and hope within a few days! I was renewed. I even felt like skipping. At that point the nutritional part didn't matter. I was abstinent!

For nine months nothing spoiled the progress of my recovery until one day I missed two meals and ate a candy bar. This relapse into highly refined carbohydrates was so like an alcohol binge that my eyes were opened wide. I could see that I was no longer able to justify a casual approach to food. Food and alcohol would keep me in a state of pain, and I no longer wished to participate.

Addictive Qualities Of Certain Foods

At that point I began to see that my problem was associated with the addictive qualities of food. I had to ask if particular kinds of food triggered loss of control. My answer was yes, certain foods triggered loss of control over the amount eaten *and* loss of control over behavior.

This incident made a good case for returning to the low carbohydrate diet. With a lot of social support in a self-help program, I was able to regain physical recovery.

Many recovering people agree with a former patient, Eileen, who says, "Today when I hear an advertisement for candy or cookies, I don't want to trade my sweet life for a sweet taste that only lasts a minute. My life goes on each day with a feeling of joy and the freedom that goes with being responsible. I have no intention of ever having to get abstinent again. It's a lot easier to *stay* abstinent than it is to *get* abstinent!"

Over the years, it was discovered that food addicts were able to tolerate certain higher carbohydrate whole foods which had not been refined or processed. In general, the foods of addiction are the sticky, pasty, greasy ones.

The processing machines do all our work for us. Instead of having to perform the work of chewing on a whole food, we can ingest lots of starch that's been through the refinement process. Be it cake or crackers or breakfast food, it's all the same — not fresh or real or whole. The body can tolerate a great deal of this refined product. Where one might limit the number of whole foods eaten, it is not possible to estimate the limit of the number of spoons of refined carbohydrate that can be eaten.

Andy shared the story of a recent binge, "I went to the grocery store and bought a box of those huge doughnuts." He formed his two hands into a circle indicating the doughnuts were about eight inches in diameter. "They were filled, glazed and frosted. I ate most of the box. All the time I was stuffing them down, I knew this was insane. Then I suffered into the night from the heartburn they caused and I finally had to take three packages of antacids to deal with the physical pain. Finally at four in the morning the heartburn calmed down." He was near tears when he continued, "And then I went back and *finished* the box of doughnuts. That was the incredible insanity of it: I couldn't stop until I'd finished them all!"

Wheat And Flour Products

Anyone who has binged on cookies, cake, pasta or crackers will wish to assess the role that starchy food plays in the addictive process. Many people are willing to accept abstinence from sugar but resist abstinence from wheat and flour-based products.

M.I.T. researcher Judith Wurtman relates the following story: "One of my clients took a businessman to a restaurant that served delicious homemade bread. While they were negotiating a tricky deal, the client passed the bread and sat back and watched as the man, initially wary, stuffed himself and mellowed in front of her eyes. She felt like a spider enticing a fly into a trap. And she made sure they shook hands on the deal while he was still under the influence of all that serotonin." (7)

"Carbohydrate consumption can also modulate other normal behaviors, increasing subjective fatigue and sleepiness, accelerating sleep onset in people with prolonged sleep latencies, diminishing sensitivity to mild pain and (in people over 40) increasing the likelihood of errors in performance tests." (8)

Recently I asked a number of individuals who abstain from sugar, why they abstain from wheat and flour-based products as well. Here is a sample of their answers:

> Abstinence from sugar alone did not relieve me from mental confusion and depression; nor was there any appreciable weight loss until I abstained from products which contain wheat and flour. — T.M.

> I abstain from wheat because it will trigger me into overeating, which results in mood swings and isolation. Also, I want to live more than I want to die. As I go on in abstinence, I feel better about myself and the mood swings have stopped. Now I like myself. — M.J.

> I abstain from food which contains wheat and flour because of the fear of what might happen if I eat it. If I eat wheat and flour products as I did in the past, I would not be able to stop . . . I recall some of the physical stress I experienced such as bloating, sick stomach, fuzzy head and the mental discomfort of wanting more. I don't want to feel that way again. I no longer debate — Can I? Can't I? — I stopped because I was told to. I experienced positive results. Why mess with success? I won't use my body as a guinea pig to see if I can eat it. — D.B.

> I abstain from food which contains wheat and flour because I have learned that, along with sugar, all are mood-altering chemicals for me. I have physical and emotional reactions. When I eat any of them, I feel angry, tired, severely depressed, I put on weight instantly, I can't think clearly and I hate people and want to be alone. Then I suffer from extreme loneliness. When I abstain, I don't experience these symptoms. — M.J.

I don't eat anything that contains sugar, wheat or flour because my body cannot tolerate them. I crave more as soon as I eat them. Then I binge. — *S.J.*

I have been able to maintain one-and-a-half years of total abstinence by not eating food that contains flour and wheat. Prior to this, the longest abstinence I had was three weeks. The compulsion and desire to eat those substances has completely gone. I don't want to add them back into my food plan because I like my abstinence. — *L.C.*

Wheat and flour are the substances I use when I don't want to feel. They are my drugs. Sugar and fats are also. — *K.B.*

If I use wheat and flour, I experience depression and suicidal thoughts. I get fat, retain water, have migraine headaches, large masses of cellulite and joint pain. All very good reasons to abstain completely. — *J.C.*

Flour and wheat-based foods cause a craving for more in my body. I can eat a whole loaf of wheat bread (sometimes two loaves) and not stop until the bread is gone. — *L.D.*

When I abstained from wheat and flour in every form, I began to feel so much better. I plan to continue this abstinence. — *S.B.*

My husband and I started an abstinence program. People get abstinent in droves. As soon as they put down food containing sugar and flour the compulsion to binge starts to subside. — *S.D.*

Eileen relates: I got sober in AA seven years before I discovered my food addiction. Even though I had a great deal of change in those seven years, I was depressed and getting more and more suicidal, unable to have an intimate relationship with anyone, not even God. Filled with anger and fear, I was so depressed that there appeared to be no solution in sight. I did everything the AA program told me to do, following directions exactly. I even had many years of therapy. The suicidal depression continued. Finally I said a desperate prayer, "God, please, please help me so I don't kill myself." After that I heard a woman tell me the truth. The solution — total abstinence from all products containing sugar, flour and wheat. When I heard her say that, I knew with my whole being that it was the answer I had been praying for.

"Ancient associations between emotional state and food consumption continue to be of interest at the present time. The connections between the two have increasingly been recognized to be of relevance to the field of psychiatry. This is, in part, a result of the need to understand and treat effectively the growing population of patients going to clinicians with eating disorders, affective disorders or both. And in part it is a result of an eruption of knowledge in neurophysiology and psychobiology of brain function and dysfunction over the last several years. Even though there is still much to be explored, it has become apparent from clinical and experimental research that there is indeed a relationship between eating and mood in many . . . people." (9)

Darla calls wheat and flour-based food "the other killers" in her life! She goes on to say:

I always knew that sugar played an important role in my life. I couldn't live without it. As a child, all the rewards for being good were in the form of sugar — a lollipop, chocolates, ice cream and so on. At age seven, a doctor put me on my first diet. He gave me pills which I later learned were amphetamines. All the food with sugar in it was taken away from me. It worked and I lost weight.

All of my life, I went from one diet to another — always losing and gaining, losing and gaining, and always feeling like a failure. Binge food always took me back to insanity.

I had a capacity for food that was unbelievable to others. I remember being so embarrassed at what I could consume that I learned to eat before and after every meal. I would make three pounds of spaghetti for my family, two adults and four small children. At least one pound went before dinner and whatever was left over from dinner was mine. I always said bread was my weakness. I would rather have a good loaf of bread and butter than cake any day.

My kids always got hot cereal, not cold cereal like other kids. I was a "good mother" and made huge pots of hot wheat cereal every morning. After they went to school and I was alone, I would have my orgy. All of that cereal and a loaf of bread comprised my breakfast. Lunch consisted of sandwiches. I could eat anything as long as I put it between two slices of bread. I used to keep boxes of a macaroni product hidden all over my kitchen for emergencies. There was a time when I thought it was my favorite food.

During all of my adult life, my weight fluctuated between 135 and 280 pounds. When I went to my first treatment center for eating disorders at age 57, I learned that sugar is addictive and once all sugar was out of my system, I would not crave food. I could then work on issues that were "eating me." I went home after 28 days feeling great. No sugar — my body was clean of it and I thought I had it licked once and for all. I was on a healthy eating program and could proceed to lose weight.

Breakfast was great. I made a beautiful plate of food every morning. After all, I was important and my food should taste good and be attractive to the eye! A leaf of lettuce with a scoop of cottage cheese in the center and all around were cubes of diet gelatin and dry wheat cereal. I would savor the chewing sensation of each little biscuit. Imagine — sugar free — and yet what a nice meal. I would dream of wheat cereal all day and couldn't wait until the next day's breakfast came.

I remember telling my Overeaters Anonymous sponsor that I did not understand how people at meetings could say that the obsession with food had been lifted and that food was no longer a problem. This was not happening for me. I had to "white knuckle" my food plan constantly.

Life went on, not well, but somewhat better. I thought OA was for the birds but I liked my sponsor so I went to a few meetings, though with a negative attitude. Finally I dropped out. My issues were stuffed, my relationships got worse but I had it licked — I was sugar free! This was a miracle to me but it was not easy. My portions were no longer measured and I remember that my first binge was a whole box of that wheat cereal.

My mother died soon after and all the feelings of guilt, remorse and regrets were too much to handle without the help of my best friend — food. I went back to eating *big time*. Within a few months I gained over 40 pounds and was totally insane. I can remember my nightly binges. My husband would leave for work at 6:00 p.m. and I was home alone. I started then. The pot came out and the spaghetti went in. I would be shaking so badly and couldn't wait until the spaghetti was cooked. I would eat five or six slices of bread while waiting. I would put butter and catsup on the spaghetti and eat it all. After that I would eat a box of the macaroni product I favored plus more bread. Some of the shaking would stop, but in a short while it would start again.

Now I yearned for sweets. I would take the car and go to the store to buy at least 10 pounds of fruit, a large bag of chocolate cookies and three pints of ice cream. A bag of gummy bears finished off the shopping expedition. By the time I got home, half the fruit was gone and I would eat the remainder, the gummy bears and follow that with the ice cream — all but half of one container which, like a good wife, I would leave for my husband. I would methodically keep track of the weight of the food I was eating. It usually weighed over 20 pounds. I would crawl into bed and use pillows to support my belly. I would take a handful of laxatives and diuretics and cry myself to sleep. I did this from the end of April until August, when I went to a different treatment center. It was either that or a mental hospital. I could not exist at home any longer. I had started abusing tranquilizers in addition to purging with laxatives and diuretics. I wanted to die.

At the treatment center I was taken off all sugar and also wheat, flour and caffeine. After the first week I stopped crying and began to believe that there might be a little hope for me. It was explained to me that people suffering from food addiction cannot handle flour or wheat either. I remember that as a child I had asthma and was skin tested many times. Wheat showed violent reactions. The doctors didn't pay much attention to food allergies and it was forgotten. My asthma left me and then came back years later after my first child was born. Again I was skin tested for allergies. Wheat raised a huge welt on my skin that stayed sore for days. At that time I was told to be aware of it.

As I look back, I cannot remember a time when I was not obsessed with food. I have always been fat, always dealing with health problems, always a poor risk for health insurance. I can honestly say that these last eight months have been the most sane and obsession-free months of my life. I have been without sugar, flour, wheat and caffeine for almost nine months. Both my eating and my weight are fine. I write a weekly food plan and make a commitment to eat according to that plan. After that, I can go about the business of living.

I am truly obsession free and can look at life in all its beauty. I have the freedom to choose how to live life, one day at a time. Each day is truly a gift from God. At age 59, I am finally free.

Darla's story shows that we can never be casual about another's treatment or recovery. With the correct information, she has been able to gain and maintain good abstinence from all mood-altering substances — food and chemicals.

Consequences Of
Food Addiction

*C*he medical and emotional consequences of food addiction have a heavy impact upon the family, society and industry, as well as the afflicted individual. Just as other addictions affect society, food addiction must be considered as a major factor in high mortality rates, lost time from the workplace, family disruption, emotional dysfunction and the usual problems associated with chronic illness. Popular and medical recognition of the severity of the problem is in its infancy.

The food addict suffers serious consequences from this affliction. A high percentage of food addicts are obese. An increase in body weight of 20% or more above desirable body weight constitutes an established health hazard. (1)

Since denial and delusion play a part in every addiction, food addicts often cannot judge size or weight realistically.

A case in point is the 500-plus-pound patient who was so deluded about her size she did not realize how huge she had become. When she was confronted by her own image in a mirror, she thought she was seeing her obese aunt standing there. On the other end of the continuum are those individuals who so fear overweight that obsession with the scales and weight result. For the food-addicted individual, dieting, fasting or purging has to pay off with weight loss. During the course of the disease, food addicts will vacillate between denial of weight gain and obsession about weight loss.

"About one fourth of all U.S. children are overweight, and these children tend to become obese adults, who in turn tend to raise children who become obese." (2) Childhood obesity has become an issue of national concern. Currently it is a popular concept to blame television for the problem. Although television encourages inactivity, it does not *cause* food addiction, it *enhances* it. The food-addicted child will find television very seductive. TV requires very little output of energy and provides the perfect atmosphere for munching. TV fuels the obsessive thoughts of food. Many advertisers use the words of addiction: Hamburgers attack us, cakes call our names, ice cream bon bons cause us to turn down dates with diplomats. "I ate the whole thing!" means "I lost control."

Children as young as eight and nine years old are dieting, scared of being fat and ridiculed. A business colleague confided that he was concerned that his eight-year-old daughter had been placed on a reducing diet. The daughter told him of her fear of the diet, stating that, "Food is my best friend." What a painful dilemma for a small child to be so involved with food and weight loss at such a young age.

Equally horrible, preteens are purging by vomiting in order to binge and stay thin. Researcher Joel Killen, Ph.D., found that 22% of (10th grade) females reported frequent dieting; 30% said they dieted occasionally and 10% engaged in total fasts. Killen also found that binging and purging occurs among substantial numbers of younger children and adolescents: 9% of nine- and ten-year-old girls in one study reported some purging behavior; 10.6% of 15 year olds vomited to control weight, 8.3% used diet pills and 6.8% used laxatives. (3) "The second National Health and Nutrition Examination Survey found that 26% of U.S. adults, or about 34 million people aged 20 to 75 years, are overweight." (4)

Medical Complications Caused By Obesity

In treating food addiction, we have observed its effects on the physical health of our patients in the form of myriad medical complications. "The major diseases associated with obesity are hypertension, atherosclerosis and diabetes, as well as certain types of cancer. Less well-known complications include hepatic steatosis, gallbladder disease, pulmonary function impairment, endocrine abnormalities, obstetric complications, trauma to the weight-bearing joints, gout, cutaneous disease, proteinuria, increased hemoglobin concentration and possibly immunologic impairment." (5)

Obesity affects the cardiovascular system by increasing the rate of heart disease. This increased occurrence of heart disease is because the obese person's heart works harder: The heart walls are thicker and larger, causing the need for more blood. High levels of fat (cholesterol) are found in the blood. This causes hardening of the arteries. The obese person risks development of blood clots. According to the National Institute of Health's 1985 report, "The Framingham Study, a large general population-based study that is strengthened by having long duration follow-up data, recently disclosed an increasing risk of this (coronary heart) disease with increasing levels of obesity, independent of the other standard risk factors." (6)

"The disease associated with the highest mortality ratios among persons who were overweight in both sexes was diabetes . . ." (7) Dr. George Cahill, Chief of the Joslin Diabetes Research Center in Boston, recently stressed the catalytic role of overeating saying, "Overnutrition unmasks the diabetic. The greatest portion of diabetes we have here in this country is frankly due just to over-nutrition. Some researchers also suspect that diabetes can be promoted by a sugar-laden diet." (8)

Respiratory problems of the obese include shortness of breath with activity, short and shallow respiration and lung stiffness. "Studies on airway resistance, lung compliance and oxygen consumption during breathing have shown abnormalities." (9) Sleep apnea occurs among food addicts, leading to unexpected death during sleep.

The obese food addict may encounter abdominal pain due to gallstones. Bile, which is supersaturated with cholesterol, hardens to form gallstones. Surgery increases the risk of heart, lung and clot complications. Life insurance statistics show that obesity increases the risk of dying from gallbladder disease. (10)

Hypertension (increased blood pressure) has been a commonly observed complication of obesity among our patients which, if untreated, may lead to stroke. According to National Health and Nutrition Examination Surveys, "The prevalence of hypertension (blood pressure greater than 160/96 mm Hg) is 2.9 times higher for overweight than for nonoverweight persons. The prevalence is 5.6 times higher for the young (20 through 44 years old) overweight than for the nonoverweight persons in this age group." (11)

Varicose veins, a health problem in this population, are due to the increased cardiac work load and the decreased output. The increase of pressure in the veins due to the increased blood pressure and increased weight all work to create varicose veins.

"An increase in body weight might be expected to add additional trauma to the weight-carrying joints, thereby accelerating the development of osteoarthritis . . ." (12) "Obesity is also associated with an increased risk of gout." (13)

According to The American Cancer Society study, "Overweight men had a higher mortality rate from colo-rectal and prostate cancer. Overweight women had significantly higher mortality rates from cancer of the gall-bladder and biliary passages, breasts, cervix, endomitrium, uterus, unspecified and ovary." (14)

Thirty years of information from the Framingham Study shows clear indications of increased rates of death for both overweight men and women. "The Framingham data gives no indication that there is a 'safe' level of overweight, that weight gain after middle age is 'healthy' or that 'desirable' weights increase with age." (15)

Some of the physical problems we have encountered in hospital patients brought about by frequent vomiting, laxative abuse and abuse of diuretics are skin problems, including dryness, rash and pimples. Swelling, pain and tenderness of the salivary glands, which give a chipmunk-like look, is a problem peculiar to the purger who vomits. Due to insufficient fiber and fluid and laxative abuse, the purger is often constipated and dehydrated.

Excessive vomiting, fasting and abuse of diuretics and laxatives lead to malnutrition, electrolyte imbalance, "Heart damage, failure of the endocrine system, infarction and perforation of the stomach after acute dilatation, multiple suicide attempts, aspiration, injury or rupture of the esophagus, severe bleeding per rectum causing anemia due to laxative abuse, hypokalemic nephropathy, depressive disorders due to starvation and severe erosion of the enamel of the teeth resulting in extensive loss of teeth." (16)

Purgers experience tooth decay due to their inadequate diet, frequent vomiting and abnormally high carbohydrate intake. Other discomforts produced by purging are bloating, edema, abdominal pain and uncomfortable feelings of fullness after eating. We have identified amenorrhea among the purging population. This lack of menstrual periods may be due to lack of body fat, rigorous athletic pursuits and reduced estrogen levels created by starving. Such women run the risk of osteoporosis.

Excessive vomiting can lead to bleeding of the esophagus. Many purgers seek treatment when this alarming condition occurs. "In an advanced stage of vomiting, the patient loses all control of the sphincter between the esophagus and the stomach." (17) This condition results in spontaneous vomiting. Patients with a long-term history of binge-purging report reaching that stage where they no longer have to induce vomiting.

Effects Of Food Addiction On Emotional Life

As we examine the problems associated with food addiction we need to recall that these problems do not occur singly. "Obesity creates an enormous psychological burden. In fact, in terms of suffering, this burden may be the greatest adverse effect of obesity." (18)

The food addict's life becomes so unmanageable and chaotic as the negative consequences of the addiction add up that desperate measures are undertaken to find a way out. Those ways out are three: insanity, death or recovery. Seventeen percent of the first 700 respondents to a survey aimed at food addicts, which is being conducted by the Florida Institute of Technology, admit that they have *attempted suicide*. (19) Death is the way out for many, whether it occurs by natural causes or by the desperate act of suicide.

"After preoccupations with eating, dieting and weight, depressive symptoms are most prominent with bulimia." (20) "Depression and anxiety are common, as are intense feelings of guilt, shame and self-contempt." (21) In the course of my employment as a food addictions clinician, the review of hundreds of standardized assessments agrees with those findings.

Food addiction affects the very spirit of the sufferer, who progressively sacrifices all that is good in life to the addiction. "I was too busy to care about my kids. My mind was so preoccupied with food that I was just too busy to care about any relationships," said Marcia.

Food addiction affects the spiritual life as it progresses and erodes values, attitudes and beliefs. How can that be? How can inanimate food bring about fundamental changes in our behavior, minds and spirit? We're no longer surprised that alcohol can adversely affect the life of the alcoholic, nor are we surprised that cocaine will create havoc in the life of the addict. But food? That's pretty hard to imagine.

Janine gives us a picture of food addiction in her story of the progression of the disease in her life after she began her recovery from alcoholism:

My earliest recollection of compulsive eating was as a toddler before I started school. I discovered the things Mother's cupboards contained. I loved the things I found there. Mother kept baking ingredients in a lower cabinet in the kitchen and within reach in the refrigerator. When she was in another part of the house, I would sneak into the kitchen for nips out of the syrup bottle, tastes of chocolate chips and hunks of brown sugar out of the box. While I was helping myself, I was feeling the fear of being found out. I liked candy, cookies and such but our meals were well balanced and sweets were very limited. I never thought that I got enough sweets. World War II rationing was an issue in my home and sweets, even gum, were rationed by the top sergeant (Mom).

In junior high and high school, I discovered junk food and always preferred it to nutritious food. I would skip meals in the lunch room and go to the drugstore for a shake or an ice cream float. By now I had quite a list of binge foods including shakes, root beer floats, bologna, canned spaghetti, french fries, shrimp cocktails, candy, cake, pie and so on. I would go from one to another as if searching for the right fix.

I wasn't overweight yet but I was big boned and grew early, so I was bigger than most of the other girls all through grade school and junior high. I was superconscious of my weight and saw myself as BIG. I quit eating breakfast, having only occasional toast on my way through the door. Lunch was junk and supper was usually a balanced meal at home, but often on the run. I was physically very active with gymnastics, dancing and high school athletics. I weighed myself on the bathroom scales at home almost daily and any chance I had at school. When I gained, I would cut down on food and increase my exercise immediately.

When I married, it became open season on sugars. The kitchen was stocked with lots of chocolate, brown sugar and marshmallows, which I nibbled on frequently. Meals were reasonable but desserts such as pies and cakes gradually increased.

Then I became pregnant and what an appetite I had! When someone said I was eating for two, I took that literally and doubled my intake of food by eating the same meals but increasing sweets. The doctor warned me about weight gain so I'd starve for days before an appointment and hit the candy bars as soon as I left his office. Somehow I maintained a reasonable weight throughout two pregnancies and a miscarriage, but my eating habits were really bad and getting worse. I gained over 50 pounds with the third child and six weeks after delivery was given a prescription for diet pills. I took them for the next 15 or more years. I used the pills for appetite control and for the way they made me feel. I was afraid I would blow up if I stopped taking them. I needed them for the energy boost. The amphetamines helped predetermine my mood and behavior. I felt higher and moved faster when I had them. Yet my eating habits deteriorated further.

Excessive drinking became part of the pattern. Mixed with the pills, I chemically controlled my moods and activities. While my kids were growing up, I used alcohol, pills, smoking, excessive activities and exercise in an attempt to play one addiction off against the other to keep my life in control and to maintain my weight. I became obsessed with keeping my figure. One time I gained 10 pounds and lost it on a popular diet while I drank bourbon in diet soda or grapefruit juice.

When I got sober (no alcohol) and 20 pounds heavier in one year, I was told not to take diet pills by members of my recovery program. When I stopped the pills, I gained 10 pounds more. At that time my eating habits included increasingly more sweets and starches. Meals were a little more regular and nutritious. Later I gradually lost interest in cooking and relied more on eating out, convenience foods and junk food. When I quit smoking three years ago, I gained 20 pounds more. In the past 11 years I've been in weight loss programs several times, losing varying amounts of weight, then regaining them. I went to a diet center two times, to another system once and also tried a variety of fad diets, several times using over-the-counter diet pills. The result was always to lose and gain.

Triggers to return to binging always started with dishonesty about what I was doing as I increased the quantity and kinds of foods I ate. When I was on binges I would start with a small amount of chocolate or other sweets, then starches which would trigger more binging.

I hid my eating from my husband for five or six years. During that time, I became more and more compulsive about eating and was obsessed with food. When I walked into a room full of people where refreshments were served, my focus was entirely on the food — how to get by the people, get to the food, and get as much as I could without being noticed! After the party, I didn't remember the people but I always remembered what food was served.

I'm sure the effect of the sweets and starches in my system affected my attitude and behavior at work. I had cravings in the morning and felt sleepy in the afternoon. Then I would spend all day on an emotional roller coaster. Excessive time lost from work was definitely a result of food addiction.

My self-esteem plummeted. I felt helplessness, a sense of total failure, self-contempt, disgust, fear and hopelessness. Eating seemed to make these feelings go away temporarily. But most of the time I just felt crazy and scared. Eating resolved that, too — for a little while!

I was worried about how my health was affected. My cholesterol was too high and that is very scary. My right hip joint was painful. I experienced some breathing difficulties with exercise or physical activity. I've also had a lot of indigestion and abdominal pain in the past year so I'm worried about having gallbladder disease.

Food addiction impaired my ability to concentrate and I experienced memory loss. This impairment has caused me the embarrassment of forgotten engagements, below average work production and fear of where it will lead.

I used to have a fairly solid religious background and built a secure relationship with God in my recovery program. In the last year of active food addiction, my contact with God slowly deteriorated. I felt separated from Him. One of the Ten Commandments says, "Thou shalt have no other gods before me." I believe that when I live in any addiction, the addictive substance becomes my Higher Power, shutting out the "Sunlight of the Spirit." Food became my Higher Power

and the god I worshipped. Food determined how I felt, what
I did and who I was. That sounds terrible and I hate to admit
it but that's the way it really was.

Although I had "cash register" honesty, I was not emotionally honest. I wore a mask to hide from myself as well as
others. When I was hurt, ashamed or angry, I would get
compulsively busy. When I was sad or lonely, I would isolate.
When scared, I clowned. I covered all my feelings with a
happy, carefree and in-control image and then gorged over it.

I got so wrapped up in myself and my defensiveness. I lost
my sensitivity to others as I became increasingly intolerant
and judgmental.

My husband and I were socially isolated as a couple because
of my lethargy caused by sugar and starch consumption.
Our sex life deteriorated. A lot of that came from my feelings
of repulsion about being fat as well as the breathing difficulty
from being fat. I know that this addiction has adversely
affected my marriage in every area. I stayed up late at night
to binge and to avoid having sex with my husband. I couldn't
stand to have him see me or touch me because I was so
enraged by the weight I gained. One time he said something
about my fat. I hated him for that!

Cash register honesty stopped at our front door. In han-
dling the household money, I was dishonest and at times
secretive regarding my spending and our financial condition.
I justified it: "What difference does it make? There's nothing
he can do. I handle the money." Compulsive spending was an
issue for me too. That was another reason for guilt — binge
shopping. I was out of control in most areas of my life. There
was no order. It was as if I were bouncing off the walls of life.

As a mother, I isolated myself from the kids during the
last year that I was actively in the addiction. Avoiding the
children and their activities left more time for eating. It
breaks my heart to admit that I just didn't want to be
around them. Whenever I could arrange to be alone, I ate
the way I needed to eat.

I know that addiction has affected my career. I have been
compulsive and unpredictable. I was also a workaholic. I did
a good job on the surface but my motives were for recognition and achievement and that never seemed to be enough.
My motives were based on my own needs rather than on
what was really best for my employer. Although I planned to

make a lot of changes to improve, I know now I only got
worse in my addiction. Then I would mask the bad feelings
with food. I became more and more dishonest with others
and myself. In the last year all my behavior was compulsive,
allowing me almost total emotional isolation. I avoided issues
at work because I was scared of my own feelings. My mood
swings impaired my relationships with the staff.

The last month my energy was drained just trying to hang
on and get from one day to the next. I was a body filling a
chair. Life had lost its meaning.

In 1960 I attempted suicide. Around that time I was diag-
nosed as hypoglycemic. The doctor recommended a glass of
orange juice with two tablespoons of sugar whenever I felt
weak, dizzy and light-headed. I drank lots of it. I spent a lot
of time during that period, and periodically since, fantasizing
about running away from home and disappearing.

I drove under the influence of alcohol daily when I was
drinking — daily on sugary foods since then. I am so grateful
that I never injured anyone while I was driving in that
condition. I have a friend who was stopped for drunk driving
while she was in a hypoglycemic attack. I believe the effect of
sugar and alcohol are the same to both of us. It's true. I'd
been walking (and driving) around drunk on sugar. I'm not
happy that I'm a food addict. But I am glad that I've been able
to find a way out of this nightmare.

Janine shows how food addiction adversely affected her
family and social life, her career, marriage and even threatened her recovery from alcoholism. The disease had an
impact on her physical, emotional and spiritual health,
leaving her feeling desperate and alone. Janine's story
shows that food addiction is a disease to be taken seriously.

Methods That Fail

id you ever hear anyone say, "Well, I guess I'll stay on this diet forever!" They probably won't. Diets are like horses — you get on and you get off but you wouldn't consider staying on forever. We're always trying new diets. In fact *new* is a word you often hear associated with diets: "I'm going on this new diet on Monday." *Monday* plays a role in dieting too. There is something about that day of the week that lends itself to *starting*. Usually Sunday is a good day to start things — but not diets.

Diets

First, we need to define the term diet. We're not talking about the amount and kind of food we usually eat as our daily fare. Rather, in this context, the term refers to a reducing diet. Reducing diets limit amounts and kinds or types of food, for the purpose of weight loss. Usually, our goal is to go on a diet, lose weight — and then go back to the way we love to eat.

There is never a shortage of new diets to try. You can *always* find one in the current month's women's magazines. It's there, right next to the picture of the featured Double-Rich-Supreme-Dark-Chocolate-Cake. There is usually a new diet book at the bookstore, too. Did you ever wonder why there are so many diets around? Because none of them work. If there were one that worked, that one would be all we would ever need.

"Truly the obsession with dieting is a national problem. More discouraging are the reports which suggest that 90 to 98% of those on 'successful' weight loss diets will regain the lost weight or more when a careful two-to-five year follow-up assessment is made. Frankly, the picture represents a major cultural denial of reality." (1) Recently I polled a group of people who agreed that for them diets don't work. Interestingly, many perceived the failure as a personal one, not the diet's. Unsuccessful dieting histories left this group with a prevailing sense of failure. "Why does diet therapy fail? Typically, fewer than 3 to 5% of patients losing 13.6 kg or more can sustain such weight loss for more than two years. Behavioral or metabolic factors, originally contributing to the development of obesity, may continue to operate after a reduction of weight." (2)

I would never criticize the creators of new diets. Those diets probably work for regular people — it's the food addicts who get crazy with them. How can they work if we deprive ourselves until we reach "normal" weight and then go back to the old way of eating? Of course some diets suggest that we change our way of living and become disciplined in order to maintain our weight loss. The disease is usually triggered long before maintenance program time. Also there were times when I read right past those maintenance suggestions because I was so delighted with my weight and appearance that I decided to celebrate with binge food.

Diets treat the symptom of the disease, not the disease itself. So what does that mean? Diets treat the symptom which is being overweight. Diets do not offer a permanent solution to addiction to refined carbohydrates. When the first cause (addiction) is treated, the symptoms take care of themselves. If you treat only the symptoms, the addiction will go on forever. Historically, professionals have treated the symptoms of food addiction while ignoring the disease. We cannot judge them harshly because neither they nor we understood the nature of the problem. We saw it as one of overweight or obesity, while failing to see that the real concern was, in fact, addiction to certain foods.

Treating the symptom is somewhat like Addie's experience with the hole in her front yard. She stumbled and fell in the hole last year and broke her ankle. This year she stumbled in again and broke her leg. Last week she took another fall and broke her hip. But she's glad her problem is so easily resolved: The emergency room is nearby and she can get a plaster cast whenever she needs one. She doesn't see that she's going to die in that hole if she doesn't get it fixed.

Going off diets is never like going on. We go on diets with great fanfare and high expectations. We announce to all around, "I'm starting a new diet on Monday." That entails shopping, preparing and studying the new way of eating. We may have to schedule trips to classes, counselors, doctors and so on in order to prepare for the new diet. While going ON is loud, going OFF is very quiet. Going OFF usually starts with one bite, just a small piece of something that's not on the diet. After all, I'm back to my normal weight. I can afford to eat just a little of this. If that bite is a binge food that triggers the disease, we're back in the disease without ever knowing what happened.

Why Diets Don't Work

We Feel Deprived

We feel a sense of loss as though something we deserve was taken away and nothing has been given back in return. We feel a profound sense of the loss of our favorite foods and no one has explained why we have to give up those foods that we want so much. We're not even sure we should give them up. All those days without high carbohydrate foods are days of ultimate sacrifice. Then we go off the diet in order to get back the things our bodies crave.

Diets Perpetuate The Obsession With Food

There are diets that promote obsession with food because they are so complicated that you are cooking and eating most of the day. These plans encourage obsession by keeping the dieter constantly involved with food purchasing, preparation and consumption. Then there are the diets which provide limited amounts of food. Starvation results in obsession.

A friend of mine, a World War II veteran who had been starved as a prisoner of war for over five years, describes his obsession with food, which continues to affect him: "I swore I would never go without food again. I continue to store food wherever there is room in the house. I can't stand the idea of being hungry." Food addicts who voluntarily restrict their food intake to starvation levels set up a cycle of starving-obsessing-binging.

We Go On Diets So That We Can Go Off

We cannot effect a permanent change in our condition. I never went on a diet with the plan to stay on it for the rest of my life. When a diet provides inadequate nourishment, limited variety and is boring, we will go back to the same food and behavior that got us into trouble in the first place.

Diets Don't Identify Trigger Foods

The term food addiction implies that a physiological, biochemical reaction in the body is the basis for the craving for refined carbohydrates. This craving and its underlying bodily mechanism is parallel to the craving for alcohol that affects alcoholics. Food addicts develop tolerance to refined carbohydrates — that is, they require increasingly greater amounts to satisfy their craving. If foods which are high in refined carbohydrates are present in a reducing diet, a food addict will be unable to succeed on that program. The refined carbohydrates will trigger relapse into the addiction.

Jeannie shares:

> I was in a program that incorporated my binge food in the diet plan. I was agitated, upset and unhappy all the time I was in that program. I know I was a terrible person to be around because of my irritability. What I was trying to do at the time was to control food over which I had lost control. In other words, I was trying to do the impossible.

We have to be aware of health food stores which contain many trigger foods as well. Health food store staples often contain sweeteners, wheat products and high fat foods which will trigger the disease.

Diets Provide Inadequate Nutrition

Many diets drastically reduce daily caloric intake or remove entire food groups or actually put the body into a state of starvation. Fasting and very low daily caloric intake are inefficient methods of weight loss. Starvation sets the body up for the next binge. The body says "nutrients" and the mind says "binge." Lack of nutrition keeps us sick. It does not help us to get well. We lose pounds in order to gain pounds which maintains the vicious cycle of the addiction and the yo-yo syndrome of weight loss and weight gain.

Diets Treat The Symptom And Not The Disease

When the overweight condition is a symptom of food addiction, diets which treat the symptom and not the disease of food addiction produce temporary results at best. Diets do nothing to change obsession with food or with weight which characterizes the food addict's thinking. Since food addiction is a complicated disease which affects the individual in all areas of life — mental, emotional, spiritual and physical — recovery must occur in all those areas as well. Obviously, a reducing diet is not designed to support the individual in all these areas.

Diets Upset The Metabolism

The metabolism slows down during dieting, creating an inefficient means of weight reduction. When we are in the disease, we take in a lot of calories but our metabolism works efficiently. When we go on a diet, the body responds to the drastic decrease of calories by slowing down the metabolism. This means we burn calories at a slower rate. When we return to our old ways of eating, the metabolism stays in low gear and we gain the weight back plus some more. The yo-yo syndrome is the result of this metabolic slowdown — lose a little, gain a lot — in which we lost the battle, not the weight.

There Is No Commitment, No Support

When we're out to dinner, at a party or at a friend's house, it is often easier to go along with the crowd than to do the work and keep the discipline of the diet. There are times when we easily cave in to the pressure of friends to have just a little of this or that. "Just a little won't hurt you," they say. We're out there alone and there is no one to support us when someone says, "Oh, you can have just a little." We believe that we *can* have just a little and we're off again. There's no one to call at two in the morning when we're doing battle with the refrigerator. There is no diet counselor who will explain and help us then.

Diets Don't Address Addiction

Diets do not take into account that abstinence from the mood-altering substance (binge food) is the foundation of recovery. Recovering from an addiction is serious business, dieting is merely a pastime. Diets don't recognize powerlessness over certain foods. Surrender to the fact of addiction changes the approach to food. Once we realize that in the presence of certain foods the disease is triggered, we can understand that the job of recovery cannot be taken lightly. When I am forced to run out of my house to buy a particular food to eat before I can rest or think or sleep or deal with my family, I am addicted to that food. Diets are not about addiction. A diet will never change that feeling of being driven to get and eat that substance.

Diets Do Not Provide Accurate Information

Diets usually provide an approach to food management and rarely, if ever, addresses the nature of the disease. There's no one to answer our questions on a day-to-day basis, especially if the diet comes from a book or magazine. Even diet clubs usually convene once a week and leave us predominantly without support.

On the day my mom said, "Kay, I've given up," my reaction was, *Hold on! We can go on another diet. We can find another plan. We can figure something out.* But it wouldn't have mattered because our problem was not as simple as we thought it was all those years we struggled with food. All the groups and programs and pills that had been offered to us over the years were never going to work because we'd never been offered the right information. No one ever told us we had a progressive, chronic, fatal disease. No one ever suggested that we were addicted. Furthermore no one ever suggested abstinence from addictive foods.

Diets Only Work Early In The Disease

That is the great deception. When a diet works early in the progression of the disease of food addiction and fails to accomplish the same end years later, the result is usually self-blame and self-disgust. When I was 15 years old and went on a diet, I lost 22 pounds. I thought my life was in control, I felt terrific, looked beautiful and figured I knew how to handle this problem. Twenty years and 30 diets later, I couldn't stay on any diet for one day. The reason for that was progression. It didn't occur to me to think that the diet wouldn't work anymore because my disease had progressed. I didn't even know I had a progressive disease so I blamed myself for being a weak glutton.

Whatever diet works early in the progression doesn't work later!

The Disease Is Cunning, Powerful And Baffling

It is so difficult to see the truth of what is happening in our lives. We keep trying to explain in a logical manner all the illogical things that are happening to us. The only logical explanation is that we have lost control over food and our lives because we are powerless over food.

Every approach which treats the symptoms of food addiction and not the addiction itself is doomed to fail. As long as we are in ignorance about the disease, we will be unable to recover successfully from our addiction to binge food. Could we expect an alcoholic to just stop drinking because it is the obvious solution to the problem? Likewise we cannot expect a food addict to stay on a diet because it is the obvious solution to the problem.

We must take into account that this is a disease which is physiological in nature but which has affected the addict in every area of life. Healing must take place in every area of life, too, including the physical, emotional and spiritual, as well as in the area of human relationships with family, friends, co-workers and others. No diet can heal the pain of addiction.

Joanne says,

> When a new ladies' magazine comes out, sometimes I grab one and check out this month's new diet idea — old habits die hard! I like to sneak a peek to see if it looks interesting. I'm not going to go on it though. It would wreck my life because diets don't work for me.

Abstinence Is Different

Why do we call it abstinence when it looks like a diet? An alcoholic goes on a diet when he eliminates alcohol, just as a drug addict diets when he eliminates his drugs of choice. We just don't call that dieting, we call it abstinence from drugs and alcohol. It is the same for the food addict. We don't call it a diet because this time it's different. In abstinence we change our whole belief system from the diet mentality to a recovery attitude.

"We ask for help to abstain from those substances we crave, ever mindful of our addiction to sugar, flour and wheat. A plan of sound nutrition will nourish our bodies and allow us freedom from the insanity of the disease of food addiction." (Based on the definition of abstinence of *Food Addicts Anonymous.*)

How do we accomplish this complete shift from dieting concepts to an understanding and implementation of abstinence? First of all, we do not do it alone. With the help of other recovering people, it can be done. Many have been able to achieve and maintain abstinence from binge food. The process is simple, yet not easy. The process involves letting go of our old ideas concerning food, diets and weight and learning a new way of life.

Dealing With Obsession And Compulsion

Remember food addiction is characterized by obsession with food and weight. The first step of recovery involves dealing with these obsessive thoughts and compulsive behaviors by recognizing them. Newcomers to recovery need to take heed of the frequency of thoughts of food with the understanding that obsessive thoughts result in compulsive behavior. When we think about eating binge food, we follow through by taking that next compulsive bite of binge food. In order to stop the process, we use a recovering person who will be available to us during the hard times to talk and pray with us. Once we have completed withdrawal from high carbohydrate foods, the cravings will subside. We must continue to seek out the help of others because this lifelong problem cannot be solved overnight.

Dealing With Deprivation

Rather than feeling cheated and deprived, in abstinence we begin to see that we can get rid of the garbage in our lives. We are getting rid of something we don't want rather than losing something of value. In recovery the real value lies in the rewards of abstinence. We are given the gifts of peace of mind, release from isolation and a sane way of life in exchange for the suffering, pain and discomfort of the disease of food addiction. The price of admission into this new way of life is surrender to the fact of addiction, surrender of old ideas and surrender of our binge food. When we admit and accept that we are powerless over certain foods with addictive properties, we begin to see binge food in a different light. We stop referring to it as "goodies" and start to see that it is poison to our bodies and to our lives. I'll never call a substance that poisons my body, mind and soul "goodies." When I see binge food, I visualize a skull and cross bones — POISON!

Abstinence Is A Committed Way Of Life

In the diet days we went on and off diets like a stunt rider leaping on and off his horse. Abstinence in recovery is different. We make a daily commitment to disciplined eating. Planning, reporting, weighing and measuring introduce that disciplined way of eating. Because we live one day at a time, we make our commitment to abstinence on a daily basis. This kind of commitment constitutes the foundation of recovery. It is the beginning of a new way of life. We can string abstinent days together to live a life of recovery. In order to focus and work on today's commitment, we give up the magic and miracle cures which never worked. We must stop the search for the easy way out to make a commitment to a new way of life that works.

Abstinence Identifies Addictive Foods

With the support of other recovering people, food addicts will be able to succeed on a food plan which identifies trigger food. By beginning with a plan which eliminates all known trigger foods, the recovering person, with the help of a sponsor, can begin to identify any food which may cause problems. If binge food appears on the food plan, its use is not an option. Over the years, many of us have learned to eliminate food which presents problems for us. When we are unable to control the use of a certain food, it is essential to abstain from that food in order to recover. Remember, we are not responsible for having a disease, but we are responsible for our own recovery.

Abstinence Provides Good Nutrition

When we no longer set unrealistic goals for thinness and begin to understand that healthy bodies require good nutrition, we start to learn to trust a food plan which provides adequate nourishment. Recovery requires giving up the yo-yo way of alternating overeating with highly restricted eating. We also give up the mistaken idea that this kind of eating worked for us. Give an abstinent food plan a chance and assess the results. Try it for 90 days and then honestly look at what it is doing for you.

Treating The Disease Rather Than The Symptom

We begin with the understanding that we will be treating the disease of food addiction rather than the symptoms of the disease: weight gain and the fear of weight gain. All of the unsuccessful programs focused on weight as the problem. It never was! The real problem is the disease of food addiction. The truth is, our problems were not causing our eating. Instead, our addictive eating was causing our problems. We must attack this disease at its very core. Withdrawal and abstinence from all addictive foods are our ongoing goals.

Maintaining An Efficient Metabolic Rate

One requirement of a successful food plan is to provide adequate calories to keep the metabolism operating at an efficient rate. This concept goes against the diet mentality. Therefore, it is a difficult one to introduce to the calorie-conscious who think that food consumption must be minimal in order to lose weight. In order to win this particular war against addiction, we must give up our old ideas about calorie cutting. We wish to operate at the most efficient metabolic rate possible. According to experts, it has been estimated that any plan based on an abnormally low intake of calories is metabolically inefficient. For this reason, a successful food plan must incorporate adequate daily caloric intake combined with adequate exercise.

Permanent Change And Freedom

Food addicts who are committed to an abstinent way of life can stop shopping for a new diet or a new program to resolve the problems associated with the addiction. Life will level off with the permanent change of abstinence. We no longer experience the emotional swings — new hope born each time we try a new diet and the crashing sense of lost hope and failure when we discover it didn't work. When we follow the path of abstinence, the results become pleasantly predictable. Trusting a reliable food plan gives us freedom from concerns regarding food.

My friend Nancy says, "I love the freedom from binging and obsessing about food. I'm grateful for this way of eating." Margie adds, "Consider the time it took to obsess, binge and vomit and you'll realize that recovery is a real timesaver. Finally I'm really free to live again. The addiction took all my time and attention." Abstinence frees us from that painful search to find a way that works. Our recovery program is the last house on the street. There is no place else to go.

The abstinent way of life offers many varieties of wholesome food, adequate nutrients and ease of selection. Recently a friend decided to pay closer than usual attention to my food selection. She said, "Why, you can eat anywhere! You just have to be specific when you order." The joy of abstinence is that we don't have to stare and drool over the other guy's meat and potato meal, we order meat and potatoes too. We just have to be conscientious about ordering a meal which has been prepared according to our needs as recovering food addicts. Fortunately, we don't have to drag powders or blenders or concoctions around with us. A food plan is really a sensible way of eating. An abstinent person's dinner wouldn't look unusual to a passerby.

The members of 12-Step recovery programs provide support by being available for sponsorship, friendship, sharing and caring. Close associations are formed in these programs where the slogan is *You can't keep it unless you give it away.* Telephone contact is numbered among the tools of recovery. Many relapses have been averted by a phone call. Newcomers are encouraged to take many phone numbers in order to ensure contact with another member in time of need. Also new members are encouraged to report their food plan to a food sponsor on a daily basis. Step sponsors provide guidance through the 12 Steps of Recovery. This kind of service, freely given, makes the 12-Step programs successful in the fight against addiction.

Most important is the fundamental fact that abstinence from addictive chemicals is the basic tool of recovery from all addictions. Recovering alcoholics abstain from alcohol and all other mood-altering drugs. Recovering narcotics addicts abstain from narcotics and all other mood-altering drugs. Food addicts abstain from binge food and all other mood-altering drugs. Addiction is addiction — only the substance is different. When the substance is food, we get thrown off course and think the solution is different. The 12 Steps are the solution which lead all sufferers of addiction out of the pain. Abstinence is the foundation of those steps.

Accurate information is crucial to recovery. Food addicts cannot make good decisions regarding recovery without accurate information about the disease. No wonder so many treat the problem lightly, thinking it is merely a problem of cosmetics. In order to do the work necessary to obtain and maintain abstinence, food addicts must understand this is a progressive, chronic, fatal illness which requires daily attention to recovery. This disease cannot be resolved by applying diet principles. A lifetime of application of the recovery principles is the method of resolution for this addiction.

We go from denial to admission. Addiction is the disease which tells us we don't have a disease. This is what makes it so cunning, powerful and baffling. After trying every method conceivable to control the disease, our recovery programs tell us that we are powerless over food. What a painful admission! When we surrender to the fact that we are powerless over certain kinds of food and because of that our life has become unmanageable, then recovery begins. Upon that admission we begin to see that our behavior made sense after all. All the loony things we did — binging, purging, dieting, stealing, lying, cheating — were about our addiction to food. With this first step we begin to walk out of the disease into recovery.

A Lifetime
Eating Plan

$\mathcal{B}$asic abstinence from all mood-altering chemicals including refined carbohydrates also includes abstinence from all sugar, flour and wheat products and food with high fat content. The following food plan is a sugar- and flour-free eating plan. It eliminates the basic components of our binge foods. This food plan is a guideline to committed abstinence.

If any of your binge foods appear on this plan, please eliminate them as a choice for you. We cannot stop binging if we continue to ingest binge foods.

We absolutely avoid all forms of sugar: sucrose, fructose, corn sweeteners, dextrose, honey, molasses, syrup and fruit juice sweetened products. We abstain from all foods containing sugar such as soft drinks, cereal, seasonings, sauces, candy, ice cream, pastries, pudding, doughnuts and cakes, as well as all hidden sugars which appear on the labels of canned, frozen and other prepared and processed foods. Low calorie and "lite" products are not usually sugar-free. The list of ingredients on the labels of diet products should be checked carefully to ensure that they are free of sugar and wheat.

We abstain from all forms of flour: macaroni, noodles, bread, pizza, crackers, bagels and pita bread, including the whole grain varieties as well as the flour in prepared foods such as gravy and sauces. This category includes all grains which have been through the refinement process, including cornstarch. It does not include the unrefined grains which you will find described in the list of abstinent food. Soy sauce contains wheat and is avoided; wheat-free tamari sauce is an acceptable substitute. (Note that not all tamari is wheat-free. Read the label to ensure that it does not contain wheat.)

Watch for flour within products, especially wheat and cornstarch. Remember that all gravy recipes include some kind of starchy thickener and therefore should be avoided.

Eliminate all high-fat foods such as nuts and fried foods including potato chips and french fries. Eliminate foods that are high in animal fat such as ice cream, butter, half-and-half, whipping cream, hard cheese, cream cheese, whole milk and 4% fat dairy products.

Avoid all forms of chocolate and cocoa including the sugar-free desserts and drinks.

Abstain from all alcoholic beverages due to the high sugar and grain content and because alcohol itself is a highly refined carbohydrate product. Food addicts risk triggering the disease with the use of all alcoholic beverages.

We do not use any medications, prescriptions or over-the-counter drugs that contain sugar. Check the label if you are purchasing medications at the drug store. Ask your doctor to check prescriptions for sugar content.

We can speculate that since the amino acids in protein blocks the production of brain serotonin, careful combination of protein with carbohydrates is essential to the food addict's food plan. It is important to maintain balance between foods high in protein and carbohydrate. This plan is based on an effective balance between the two which has proven successful for food-addicted individuals in controlled hospital settings.

This food plan provides relief from day-to-day concerns about food and diet. Learning to trust the food plan takes time. Use it on a daily basis, eating no more and no less than is suggested. We no longer choose to be hungry in order to be thin. The results will be amazing. One of the pitfalls of abstinence is the concern about the large amount of food in the food plan. Do not cut back on the amount of food prescribed. It is necessary to avoid hunger in order to avoid binging again. The food plan will ensure relief from obsessive/compulsive eating. Learn to trust it and enjoy the freedom.

Variety in food choices is important to keep the food plan interesting. Using one food too frequently may indicate that it is a binge food.

Be aware that there are variations of food plans, including some that are more conservative and others less so. If your treatment center or sponsor has provided you with a plan based on abstinence from all addictive food and that plan is working for you, stay with it.

Before using this food plan, check with your physician for approval.

Table 8.1. Daily Portions

Breakfast	Lunch	Dinner	Before Bed	Daily
1 Dairy	1 Protein	1 Protein	1 Dairy	1 T. Oil
1 Protein	1 Raw Vegetable	1 Raw Vegetable	1 Fruit	1 oz. Sauce*
1 Grain	1 Cooked Vegetable	1 Cooked Vegetable		1 T. Spice*
1 Fruit		1 Starchy Vegetable or Grain		6 Servings Sweetener*

*Optional

Table 8.2. Daily Portions for Men

PROTEIN — 5 oz. red meat, 6 oz. turkey, chicken, veal, fish

STARCH —   starchy vegetable or grain at lunch

FRUIT —   evening meal

OIL —   add 1 tablespoon per day

Abstinent Food List

Protein	One Serving
Beef	4 ounces
Veal	4 ounces
Pork	4 ounces
Lamb	4 ounces
Chicken	4 ounces
Turkey	4 ounces
Fish	4 ounces
Shellfish	4 ounces
Soy Protein (tofu)	4 ounces
Eggs	2 medium
Legumes (cooked)	1 cup
Buttermilk	1 cup
Yogurt (low fat)	1 cup
Milk (skim or low fat)	1 cup
Cottage cheese (low fat)	½ cup

Include chicken or fish in your food plan frequently. Limit heavier meat (beef, pork and lamb) to three times per week. Individuals with elevated cholesterol will wish to avoid or restrict red meat and eggs. (Egg lovers may cook one whole egg plus two egg whites to decrease the amount of cholesterol intake.)

One-half cup of egg substitute may be used. Check the list of ingredients before using.

Soy protein such as tofu can be used to add variety to your menus. Tofu is a bland product which absorbs the flavors of the foods or spices with which it is cooked or blended. It can be added to stews, soups or casseroles to boost the protein content. Tofu is an excellent protein around which vegetarian menus can be planned.

All visible fat should be removed from meat and poultry. Purchase the leanest products available. It is acceptable to eat chicken skin but many abstainers prefer to remove it. If you wish to eat the skin, cook the chicken in such a way (for example, broiling) to ensure that the fat underneath the skin cooks away.

Protein preparation will include baking, broiling, grilling or pan frying in no-stick cooking spray.

It is possible to design good protein vegetarian menus around legumes, which include split peas, soy products, lima beans, red beans, pinto beans, navy beans, lentils, kidney beans, Great Northern beans, chickpeas, blackeyed peas and black beans. Vegetarian menus also may rely on the use of dairy products for protein portions. These products should be included in the food plan for variety in the selection of protein.

Limit processed foods that are high in sodium and fat content such as hot dogs and cold cuts. Read labels on smoked meat products such as ham to ensure that they are sugar-free.

If you wish to increase calcium intake and decrease protein in your diet, use dairy products to replace some animal protein. Other good sources of calcium are soybeans, salmon and dried beans. (1)

Vegetables: Choose 1 cup servings from the following:

Artichoke (not marinated in oil)	Mushrooms
Asparagus	Okra
Bamboo shoots	Onions
Beans: yellow or green	Parsley
Beets	Peppers: green or red
Belgian Endives	Pickles, dill
Bok choy	Pimentos
Broccoli	Radishes
Brussels sprouts	Romaine
Cabbage	Rutabaga
Carrots	Sauerkraut
Cauliflower	Snowpeas
Celery	Spinach
Chicory	Sprouts
Chinese cabbage	Summer squash
Cucumber	Tomato, tomato juice
Eggplant	Turnip
Endive	Vegetable juice
Escarole	Water chestnuts
Greens	Watercress
Lettuce – all varieties	Zucchini

Always include raw fresh vegetables for lunch and dinner. Do not substitute cooked vegetables for raw, although raw may be substituted for cooked. It is fine to eat two cups of raw vegetables for any meal. Salad bars provide raw vegetable meals. (A word of caution about salad bars: Avoid combination salads. Such dishes as carrot salad, three bean salad and marinated vegetable combinations contain sugar. Also it is difficult to estimate the amount of salad dressing used.) The salad bar is a good place to *keep it simple* by selecting combinations of plain raw vegetables. This will ensure abstinence.

Frozen or canned vegetables are acceptable unless sugar has been added. Read the label. You may find sugar lurking in the strangest places. Canned vegetables must be inspected carefully as sugar is often added.

You may wish to select low sodium products. If you are concerned about the sodium content, avoid pickles, sauerkraut and vegetable juices unless marked "low sodium." Canned vegetables usually contain added sodium in the form of salt. One cup of sugar-free tomato juice or vegetable cocktail may be used as a cooked vegetable serving.

Vegetables are an excellent source of vitamins, minerals and fiber. Steam or cook them in small amounts of liquid to ensure retention of nutrients. If you discard the liquid from canned vegetables, you are discarding the nutrients which have been cooked out. Vegetables that are purchased fresh and kept refrigerated are the best choice for nutrition.

Have fun with vegetables. The beautiful colors help create sensational dishes. Pureed cooked vegetables make lovely sauces for meat, fish or fowl. Be creative with salad dishes. We tend to rely on lettuce as the foundation of most salads. Introduce the dark leafy vegetables for variety in appearance and taste. Plan to have an assortment of raw chunky vegetables frequently instead of lettuce salad. It's possible to keep the food plan fun and interesting if you keep the menu varied.

Fruit: Choose one serving portion from the following:

Apple	1 medium
Apple juice	½ cup
Applesauce (sugar-free)	½ cup
Apricots	3 medium
Berries	1 cup
Cantaloupe	½ medium
Cranberry juice (sugar-free)	1 cup
Fruit cocktail (canned in juice)	½ cup
Grapefruit	½ large
Grapefruit juice	1 cup
Honeydew	¼ medium

Kiwi	3 average
Lemons, limes	3 small
Nectarine	1 large
Orange	1 large
Orange juice	1 cup
Peach	1 large
Pear	1 large
Pineapple	1 cup
Pineapple juice	1 cup
Plums	3 medium
Prune juice	1 cup
Rhubarb	1 cup
Tangerines	2 small
Watermelon (diced)	1 cup

Fresh, frozen or canned fruit products are acceptable as long as no sugar has been added. It is crucial to read the list of ingredients to be sure that the products are sugar-free.

Fruit is a good source of nutrients and fiber. We favor fresh hard fruit to provide fiber and chewing action. Fruit juices lack fiber and are therefore less filling and satisfying. However, fruit juices are usually available in restaurants even when whole fruit is not. Fruit may be combined with dairy products for breakfast and at bedtime. Drain canned fruit before measuring and use juice separately.

Grains: Choose 1 cup (cooked) servings from the following:

Barley	Oat bran (1/3 cup, raw)
Brown rice	Oatmeal
Corn Grits	Puffed brown rice
Cream of rye cereal	Puffed corn
Kasha	Soy cereal
Millet	Barley

Avoid fruit juice sweetened products. There is no way to estimate the amount of fruit juice used in these products. Health food stores offer a good selection of sugar-free, wheat-free cereal products, such as corn flakes and cream of rye cereal. Cream of rye cereal looks, tastes and is prepared like oatmeal. Look for it. It is a simple way to improve variety in the food plan.

Starchy Vegetables: Choose 1 cup
(cooked) servings from the following:

Beans: lima, navy, northern, kidney, pinto
Corn: whole kernel
Parsnips
Peas: green, dried
Potato: sweet, yam, white (baked or mashed)
Pumpkin
Squash: winter, acorn, hubbard, spaghetti, butternut

Grains and vegetables that are high in starch should be measured carefully. The food plan calls for protein to be served with meals which include high carbohydrate foods. Remember to maintain the balance between protein and carbohydrate foods. It is important to the success of this plan. Arbitrary adjustment of the food plan changes its effectiveness.

Be sure to vary grains and starchy vegetables from day to day. It is important to avoid eating the same foods every day.

Starchy vegetables are prepared by boiling or steaming. Abstain from fried products such as french fries and potato chips.

Corn — fresh, frozen or canned without sugar — is acceptable. Avoid popped corn, corn bread and Mexican foods made with corn flour (shells and tortillas). It has been my observation that these corn products are used by individuals who frequently relapse.

Dairy may be used as protein.
Choose from the following:

Buttermilk .... 1 cup
Cottage cheese (1% milkfat) .... ½ cup

Milk (skim or 1% milkfat) .... 1 cup
Yogurt (low fat or non-fat) .... 1 cup

Dairy products are a major source of calcium which is needed for the health of bones and teeth. We are now aware of the need for calcium to prevent osteoporosis. Calcium also maintains regular heartbeat, alleviates insomnia, helps metabolize iron and aids the nervous system in impulse transmission. (2)

Oil: 1 tablespoon per day total

Margarine
Mayonnaise (sugar-free)
Salad dressing (sugar-free)
Vegetable oil: olive, corn, safflower

The oil allowance is 1 tablespoon per day. Any combination of oil, margarine, mayonnaise or salad dressing is allowed. For instance, 1 teaspoon of margarine for lunch and 2 teaspoons of salad dressing for dinner would equal the total daily measurement of oil. Three teaspoons equal 1 tablespoon. Mixing salad dressings or mayonnaise half and half with yogurt stretches the dressing to cover lots of salad. Do not abstain from oil. Fatty acids are necessary for good health, weight loss, soft skin and hair. (3)

Spices: 1 teaspoon per day (optional)

Some commonly used spices enhance abstinent food; use as follows:

Allspice: good on peaches and stewed fruit
Basil: delicious in stew
Bay leaf: for braised meat dishes and stew
Black pepper, coarse grind: a treat on salad and protein dishes
Caraway seed: nice flavor for salad
Celery seed or celery salt: added to cole slaw
Chili powder: sugar and wheat-free in regular chili or vegetarian chili (using tofu or beans instead of meat)

Chinese Five: for stir fry and to flavor coffee

Chives: for soup, salad and meat dishes or on baked potato topped with cottage cheese

Cinnamon: to flavor coffee or in cottage cheese mixed with fresh peaches

Curry powder: in Indian dishes

Dill: sprinkle on broiled fish

Flavored extracts: sugar and alcohol-free to flavor coffee, yogurt and cereal

Garlic: for Italian dishes and stir-fried vegetables

Ginger: use in stir-fried vegetables

Herb season mixtures: for charcoal-broiled meat and fish dishes

Maple liquid flavor: nonalcoholic to flavor cooked cereal

Mustard: dry for meat dishes and salad dressing

Nutmeg: on sliced fresh peaches

Oregano: a must for Italian dressing and dishes

Paprika: nice color and flavor for broiled fish

Parsley flakes: in salads

Sage: mixed with brown rice for turkey "dressing"

Thyme: in preparing veal and pork

Condiments: 1 ounce per day total

Check ingredients to ensure that these products are free of sugar, wheat and starch. Avoid condiments prepared with wine.

Dill Pickle Relish	Salsa
Horseradish	Tamari Sauce (wheat and alcohol free)
Ketchup (sugar-free)	Tomato Sauce
Mustard (prepared)	Vinegar, all flavors

Artificial Sweeteners: 6 servings per day

We do not advise or encourage the use of any artificial sweeteners. In the event that you elect to use them, abstain from all sugar substitutes that list nutritive sweeteners including dextrose, maltodextrin and polydextrose to name a few. (This includes all of the sweeteners currently distributed in small packets.) If you choose to use saccharine products, limit to six servings per day. The six-serving limit includes all soda, gum and all sweeteners used in cooking, coffee and tea. Be aware that sweeteners can be abused. If you react addictively to sweeteners, abstain from them. Some so-called sugar-free chewing gum contains sugar; check the list of ingredients. Just a reminder: Gum perpetuates the disease in terms of oral preoccupation and activity. Strictly limit or abstain from gum. Read labels carefully. Diet soda should list zero (0) carbohydrates and zero (0) sugar on the label.

Maintenance Plan

Who needs the maintenance plan?

1. Individuals who have achieved their ideal weight on the food plan.
2. Men who experience rapid weight loss.
3. Individuals who begin abstinence at their ideal weight or below.

Use **Daily Portions, Table 8.1** as a base, and

Level 1 • Add one starch or grain serving to lunch.
Level 2 • Increase oil to 1 tablespoon at lunch (for a total of 2 tablespoons of oil per day).
Level 3 • Add one fruit serving to any meal.
Level 4 • Add 2 ounces of protein to any meal.
Level 5 • Add 1 cup raw vegetables to any meal.

All maintenance levels depend on weight stabilization. On maintenance, plan to weigh once weekly. If you gain two pounds or more, return to the previous level. If you continue to lose, go on to the next level. If you reach level 4 and continue to lose weight, repeat the process and continue to increase intake of food at the same rate.

Managing Food

$\mathcal{P}$lanning is the key to successful implementation of the food plan. You may wish to keep track of your selections in planning a *weekly* menu. This is a discipline which serves us well in shopping and preparing our abstinent meals.

In early recovery, planning and learning go hand in hand. Remember, we are learning a way of life, not just another diet. Although there is a fine line between adherence to a food plan and rigid perfectionism, I believe we need to develop a strict approach to the food plan early in our program. We need to make it part of our daily routine. This discipline will result in the accurate use of the plan which will aid in the selection of abstinent foods. It's like learning to play the piano — we improve with practice. Individuals with long-term abstinence may wish to continue to weigh, measure and plan meals in order to ensure adherence to the food plan. Certainly there are times when we need to check our food consumption in terms of volume by weighing and measuring, no matter how long we've been abstinent. Let's call these honesty checks. Bad habits can creep in and we need to maintain vigilance and awareness of our eating behavior. I don't think that it will always be necessary to carry scales and measuring cups to restaurants, although for some it may be. Most restaurants provide moderate servings which meet our goal of eating average amounts. Early in recovery some may find it necessary to avoid "all you can eat" salad bars and buffets or you may wish to weigh and measure. At the point when you become more competent in judging the amounts of food provided on the plan, you will be comfortable about dining out without measuring and weighing.

As an active food addict I was unwilling to focus on what I was eating and I was absolutely unaware of the huge amounts I was consuming. All of that was part of the delusion of the addiction. It would have been shocking if I had actually counted the calories that I was ingesting on a daily basis. The disease progressed because I was blind to my behavior. We need to be strict about weighing and measuring when weight loss should occur and does not — and when weight gain occurs when it should not. Many individuals stop losing weight and begin to change the food plan, usually to their regret, instead of returning to weighing, measuring, recording and reporting.

Getting Started

Getting off on the right foot requires a commitment to weighing and measuring our food. Begin by investing in measuring spoons, measuring cups and a food scale. It is a good idea to have several one-tablespoon measuring spoons and four or five one-cup measuring cups. Nested measuring cups are handy. You will wish to have a separate cup for each course. Dinner will require three — one for salad, one for starch and one for the cooked vegetable.

Do yourself a favor and purchase a substantial food scale. You will be using it frequently and the lightweight ones are tippy and annoying.

Planning For The Week

Planning meals and purchasing food in advance are keys to the successful use of the food plan. It is easy to become confused about what and when to eat when one is new on the program. The following is a sample three-day plan, including shopping list. It is not suggested that you eat exactly the listed foods but use this as a guide to planning food that you and your family will enjoy.

Monday

Breakfast

1 cup pineapple
1 cup yogurt
1 cup oatmeal
1 cup milk

Lunch

1 cup chunky raw
   vegetables: tomatoes,
   cucumbers, red onions
1½ tsp. mayonnaise
1 cup cooked green beans
4 oz. tuna fish
1 glass decaf tea

Dinner

1 cup spinach salad:
   spinach, red onion,
   mushrooms
1½ tsp. oil
½ tsp. vinegar
4 oz. broiled sirloin steak
6 oz. baked potato
1 cup asparagus, plain
Bottled water with lemon

Before Bed

1 apple
1 cup skim milk

Tuesday

Breakfast

2 poached eggs
1 cup orange juice
1 cup puffed brown rice
   cereal
1 cup milk
1 cup of decaf coffee

Lunch

4 oz. roast turkey breast
1 cup tossed salad
1½ tsp. Newman's Own oil
   & vinegar salad dressing
1 cup steamed broccoli
Lemon-lime sparkling water

Dinner

1 cup homemade cole slaw
   with 1½ tsp. mayonnaise
4 oz. lemon-dill baked
   flounder
1 cup whole kernel corn
   and lima beans, mixed
1 cup cooked carrots

Before Bed

1 fresh peach
½ cup cottage cheese

Wednesday

Breakfast

2 oz. broiled sausage
1 scrambled egg
1 fresh pear
1 cup puffed corn cereal
1 cup skim milk

Lunch

Homemade vegetarian chili:
   1 cup kidney beans,
   1 cup canned tomatoes,
      pepper & onion
   1 cup tossed salad
   1½ tsp. dressing

Dinner

4 oz. roast chicken
Plain baked sweet potato
1 cup romaine lettuce
1½ tsp. Caesar salad
   dressing (sugar-free)
1 cup cooked cauliflower,
   plain
1 cup decaf tea

Before Bed

1 baked apple
1 cup buttermilk

Shopping List

Romaine lettuce: enough for two meals
Iceberg lettuce
Bagged shredded cabbage
Fresh tomatoes
Fresh cucumbers
Red onions
Fresh spinach
Fresh mushrooms
Medium sweet potatoes
Medium white baking potatoes
Green peppers
Fresh cauliflower
Fresh broccoli
Fresh lemons
Fresh apples
Fresh peaches
Fresh pears
Mayonnaise (Some sugar-free brands are available)
Newman's Own Salad Dressing: contains no animal fat, sugar or other unwanted ingredients. This is an ideal dressing for abstinent food addicts (oil and vinegar dressing only).
Caesar salad dressing
Fresh or frozen green beans: no added ingredients or sauces
Fresh or frozen asparagus: no added ingredients or sauces
Orange juice
Canned tuna fish
Pineapple canned in its own juice
Canned kidney beans
Canned tomatoes
Decaffeinated tea bags
Decaffeinated coffee: instant and automatic drip
Lemon-lime seltzer: no salt, no caffeine, no sweetener

Mineral water: lemon flavor

Cooking spray

Cooking oil

Vinegar

Lean sirloin steak

Turkey sausage: no fillers, no sugar. Be sure to read the
    label — we can't just pick up any brand of sausage.

Turkey breast: nothing added

Nonfat plain yogurt: no sugar, no fruit

Cottage cheese: 1% milkfat

Skim milk

Buttermilk

Medium eggs

Baked chicken (from deli)

Puffed brown rice cereal (from health food store or some
    grocery stores)

Puffed corn cereal (from health food store or some
    grocery stores)

Plain oatmeal: no added ingredients

Chili powder: no sugar, no wheat

You may have many things on hand that you will wish
to incorporate into your new food plan. Do not rush out
to buy a lot of new products if your cupboard contains
acceptable ones. On the other hand, many cupboards will
have to be restocked because they are laden with high
carbohydrate offerings. Clearing the cupboards of sugar-
laden food can be a family project. Often family members
will give support by assisting in this project. If some
family members insist on keeping sugary food in the
house, they may be hooked on it. Handle these situations
with care and caution. You may be confronting food addiction in family members.

Be sure to read the labels on all processed food. Sugar
shows up in the most unexpected places. Do not trust
manufacturers to *continue producing* sugar- and wheat-free
products either. Check labels and recheck. Manufacturers

may decide to add sugar or wheat to a product you've been using for many years. Check labels on all canned, frozen and packaged food.

Reading labels is crucial to abstinence. The labels of food that I buy usually include very few ingredients. Keeping it simple is the best way. *Beware:* A food can be labeled sugar-free and still contain some other unacceptable ingredients. Ignore the claims you see on the *front* of a food label. Instead, read the *fine print on the back label* which lists the ingredients.

Avoid all products that include:

White sugar	Wheat
Brown sugar	Wheat flour
Caramel color	Flour
Corn syrup	Glucose
Fructose	Sucrose
Dextrose	Molasses
Honey	Invert sugar
Maltose	Maple sugar or syrup
Food starch	Modified food starch
Alcohol	Maltodextrin
High fructose corn syrup	Turbinado sugar
Malt and Malt syrup	Fruit sweeteners
Caffeine	Rice Syrup

The FDA requires food companies to list the ingredients in a product in descending order by volume. Therefore the first ingredient listed represents the largest amount.

Reporting To A Food Sponsor

After planning comes reporting to a food sponsor. It is customary to report our day's plan to a sponsor every morning at an agreed upon time. If there is a change in our plan, we report that change, too. The reporting may sound foolish, but it is important in several ways. First, the sponsor can help us understand the food plan itself. Also reporting keeps us honest. We are not as willing to cheat when we realize we'll have to call our sponsor and report it. Talking to our sponsor on a daily basis provides support and encouragement. Don't forget, we are confronting a disease, not dieting. Plan, report, commit and let go!

Food Preparation

All food on the food plan is cooked without added fat. Beware of added fat in restaurant food. Order your food broiled dry. At home we prepare food in the oven by broiling, roasting or baking; on the stovetop by boiling, simmering, pan frying in cooking spray or poaching; in the microwave by the same methods; and on the charcoal grill. Avoid adding fat such as pork and dairy products to vegetables. Sour cream and cheese sauces are high in animal fat and are to be avoided.

If you work outside of the home, you may wish to do the major work of preparation on the weekends, simplifying preparation during the work week. Make large batches of abstinent stew (no gravy), chili and prepared raw vegetables in advance to freeze or store.

Because most commercial fast food is processed and prepared with ingredients we wish to avoid, quick meals can be really difficult. TV dinners, even the diet ones, are inappropriate for this program. You may speed meal preparation by going to a salad bar and buying cut up vegetables to add to shredded lettuce, then storing in the refrigerator in plastic sealed bowls or bags with a paper towel to absorb moisture. Remove paper towel when damp. You can store a supply of salad to last for several days. Of course, you can store raw vegetables that you have prepared yourself in this manner, too.

One time-saver that I used regularly is roasted chicken from the deli. Also since I now eat vegetarian meals, I use canned beans of all descriptions which contain no added ingredients other than water and salt.

Adjusting The Food Plan

It is suggested that you consult a sponsor when making changes in the food plan. You will wish to eliminate all binge foods as an option. Just because a particular food appears on the food plan does not mean that it will be safe for you. We have tried to eliminate common binge foods so that the food plan we present to you will be the safest possible, but there may be some danger foods on our list. We hope not! This is a very conservative food plan. Eat no more and no less than the food plan calls for unless you've spoken to a sponsor experienced in the use of this food plan. Remember, when you cut down or cut out, you are putting yourself on a diet. We know that diets don't work. When you increase your intake of food, you may be on your way to a binge.

Some special situations which need to be addressed: Vegetarians, who abstain from animal products for health, ethical or religious reasons, are never expected to eat them. The food plan offers a variety of protein choices which will be appropriate for vegetarians, such as tofu and other soy products. If you are a lacto-ovo vegetarian, you will include eggs and dairy products for protein portions. For those who have food allergies, in the event that you are allergic to anything on the food plan, eliminate those foods as a choice. You are never expected to eat anything that is detrimental to your health.

Eating In Restaurants

It takes vigilance, awareness, assertiveness and a lot of clear directions to eat abstinently in restaurants. Here is a list of directions:

No croutons on the salad
Plain baked potato without butter or sour cream
No bread or rolls
No gravy, sauces, sour cream or butter
Dry broiled protein
Salad dressing, oil and vinegar, served in cruets,
     unmixed.

I have had to return meals to the kitchen as often as three times to get them right. Sometimes I have made the error in giving the order and sometimes the server or chef has. One time, a waiter told me, "Oh, I didn't know it was a health problem. I thought you just didn't like it so I put it on anyway." That comment left me wondering!

Sometimes it is painful to assert ourselves in such a way. Often it is embarrassing and uncomfortable to make so many requests during the ordering of a meal. Frankly, I prefer it when I can order simply without lots of discussion. But I never forget that my life depends on abstinence.

Commitment is the key to success on this food plan. Make a commitment to try it for 90 days. If things are not better, you can always return to your old ways. I suspect that after 90 days, you will look better, feel better and be involved in your recovery program. We can make a commitment to recovery or to the disease. We can only have it one way.

Check Ingredients

Since the foundation of our recovery is built on physical abstinence and because we eat four times a day, it is our ongoing responsibility to check the contents of the foods that we eat. Our goal is to use only food that is free of sugar, flour, wheat and the other specific ingredients listed in our food plan. This is our personal commitment to recovery and can be achieved by planning, reading the list of ingredients and asking questions about products. Check the list of ingredients every time you purchase. Manufacturers change recipes from time to time. A product that was acceptable last week may not be so this week.

If a product you have at home is okay for abstinence, don't assume that the same product is acceptable when served in restaurants or at a friend's home. Check the ingredients. I recently checked on a soft-drink powder served in a restaurant and, although the ingredients were sugar-free in the grocery store product, the restaurant product contained maltodextrin as the second ingredient and therefore was not a good product for food addicts.

Abstain from artificial sweeteners in the packets. They all contain dextrose. Check ingredients of all sweeteners to ensure that they are sugar-free.

Read the list of ingredients when choosing rice cakes. Many of them now contain unacceptable sweeteners, flour, popcorn and cheese. *Warning:* Many food addicts report problems with plain rice cakes. If you binge on rice cakes, abstain from them.

Keep It Simple

Keep your food plan simple. Complicated mixtures of food in large batches defy accurate measurement. If recipes require mixing ingredients, measure your portion individually in the correct amounts. For instance, if you are cooking chili, mix 1 cup of beans, 1 cup of tomatoes and 4 ounces of meat for your single portion rather than trying to establish what your serving will be from a larger batch.

Be Assertive

Take charge of your restaurant meal! Order food without sauces or dressing of any kind. For risk-free eating, order dry broiled meat or fish, plain unmixed oil and vinegar for salad, salad with vegetables only (no croutons, olives or cheese) and baked potato without any added fat. Cooked vegetables are risky. They may contain added sugar and fats. Give clear directions concerning these to ensure that they are free of sweeteners, fats and other additions.

Sugarfree Or Sugarfull?

Forget the so-called "sugar-free" frozen yogurts and desserts. None of them is truly without sugar since they contain polydextrose, maltodextrose and other forms of nutritive sweetener which will trigger the disease. Read the list of ingredients instead of placing blind faith in manufacturers' claims.

ZERO Sugar

Zero sugar is the goal of our abstinence. Eliminate all forms of it. Buy or make sugar-free salad dressing. There is no way to estimate the amount of refined sugar that can be physically tolerated by a food addict, so aim for total elimination. Powdered butter substitutes are not sugar-free. Abstain from fruit juice sweetened products. There is no way to estimate the amount of fructose present in these products.

Travel

When you travel, plan ahead, be flexible, and above all take off with a firm commitment to maintain abstinence.

Here is a list of items you may wish to carry, or ship ahead when you are traveling:

Spices	Oat Bran
Salad Dressing	Can Opener
Powdered Milk	Measuring Cups
Cans of Tuna and	Measuring Spoons
Chicken	Plastic Covered Bowls
Small Cans of Fruit	Food Scale

With an ice pack you can carry perishables such as:

Cottage Cheese	Fresh Fruit
Yogurt	Fresh Vegetables

If you are traveling to foreign territories where it will be difficult to find acceptable food, mail or ship useful foods ahead.

Traveling by air? Don't count on the airlines to serve you an appropriate meal. No matter how carefully you order in advance, the quantities and preparation will not be suitable for abstinence. Eat before or after the plane ride or take your own food. Sometimes it is possible to time your trip so that you will be in an airport at mealtime.

If so, find a salad. That will be a better bet than trying to get an abstinent meal on the plane.

Under the worst circumstances, remember two cups of lettuce and a glass of low-fat milk constitutes a lunch. I hope you will never have to eat such an uninspired lunch, but I've chosen to have garden salad (no dressing) and a carton of low-fat milk when my niece and nephew wanted to have a kid's meal, served with toys, at that famous fast food place.

If you like to go prepared, two cups of raw vegetables, ten tiny rice cakes and a one cup serving of yogurt will fit into a tiny nylon bag with a little ice pack. This dinner could fit into your handbag.

Most Frequently Asked Questions About The Food Plan

How many calories per day? The food plan is based on an adequate number of calories per day. The actual calorie count fluctuates according to the kinds of food selected. For instance, 4 oz. of one kind of protein may have more calories than some other selection from the protein list. This is one reason why it is necessary to eat a variety of foods so that we will not get stuck on a particularly high or low calorie menu.

Do you count calories? This plan is not based on a specific number of calories per day. The basis of the program is abstinence from proven binge foods and weighed and measured amounts of food. Abstinence from binge food relieves us of cravings. Weighing and measuring give us freedom from concern that we've eaten too little or too much.

Is it okay to have sugar-free bacon? Bacon can be selected as a protein serving although the high-fat content should be considered. I would not choose to eat 4 oz. of bacon at a meal. One egg and 2 oz. of bacon would make a nicer breakfast. Individuals who avoid high cholesterol food would not wish to eat bacon or eggs frequently.

Why does the food plan include brown rice and not white rice? The food plan does not include any refined products. I believe that the elimination of refined products is crucial to the success of this plan.

What about holidays? At first it will seem difficult to take our focus off the food associated with holidays and focus on recovery instead. Turn to your helping network to gain support during the holidays. You will learn that gifts other than food will give joy to your loved ones, such as small toys in Easter baskets or flowers instead of hearts filled with candy. Nutritious food will begin to replace the rich and heavy food of former years. Happier in recovery, the abstinent food addict will find the holidays are more special and fulfilling.

What should I keep in the house and what should I discard? If you are concerned about keeping binge food in the house, I would suggest that you discard it. If your family members are particularly fond of your trigger foods, ask them to order those foods in restaurants so that you can keep the house free of binge food. Many times I bought highly refined food for the family and ate it all myself. Early in recovery it is safer to keep the house free of dangerous foods. Ask your family members to cooperate in this. Remember, it is crucial to plan ahead and keep supplies of abstinent food in the house.

How should I cook for the family? One way to keep it simple is to cook the same meal for the family that you eat. Their nutrition will improve if the family meal includes the protein, raw and cooked vegetables and starch that you prepare for yourself. You may wish to add bread or rolls to their meal and fresh fruit for dessert.

What about company? The abstinent menu can include many foods which are delicious when they are well prepared. In our food-addicted minds, we believe that everyone enjoys rich food. I have served completely abstinent foods at parties which everyone enjoyed.

What about dessert? We don't eat it. Dessert is one of our old ideas. Let go of it. I enjoy decaf coffee while others eat their dessert. I would never be happy with just *one* dessert. One was too many and there was never enough sweet food to satisfy my craving. I am grateful to be relieved of the need to binge on sweet desserts.

Does the food plan change when you reach an appropriate weight? Yes. See the section on Maintenance Plan. Beware that you do not try to reach and maintain too low a weight. Consult your doctor and program sponsor for guidance about a good weight for you.

How can I keep from getting bored with eating the same thing all the time? We can avoid boredom by introducing new foods into our daily plans. Try items you thought you didn't like. The palate changes during abstinence and you may be surprised to find that you really do enjoy food you've never eaten before. Many main dish recipes you enjoyed before abstinence may be adjusted to an abstinent way of preparation. For example, make stew without thickening the juice, then weigh and measure your portions of meat and vegetables.

How about taco shells made from ground corn? Ground corn is corn flour and should be excluded.

How important is it to write down the food we eat? In early recovery and in times of stress it is very important to write down what you are going to eat. The written plan which includes the weights and measurements of our food is a basic way to avoid the self-deception that is so much a part of this disease. We really don't know if we've been accurate in terms of amounts and preparation of food unless we commit our daily plan to paper.

How do you order in restaurants? Ask questions. Be assertive. Return food that is improperly prepared. Ask for *dry* broiled protein. Make simple selections from the buffet and menu such as baked or broiled protein, baked potato, salad with no croutons, cooked vegetable without sauces. Be sure to stipulate that you do not wish to have bread crumbs served on baked or broiled entrees. Ask that the salad dressing be served on the side.

How long do I have to plan and report food? This is a question best answered by a food sponsor. There are a number of variables which need to be considered when the decision to stop planning and reporting is made. (1) Are you in a good place emotionally at this time? (2) Why do you wish to discontinue? (3) Are you attending meetings consistently? (4) What step are you currently working on? Usually, a food sponsor will be glad to give you guidance in this decision.

When I am going to be away from home for several weeks at a time, what can I do to plan ahead for these occasions? You may wish to keep certain items in your room, such as a cooler for dairy products and fruit. When traveling, the two major problems are (1) finding dairy and fruit for the evening snack and (2) finding an abstinent grain for breakfast. Also follow the hints for ordering in restaurants.

Do I always have to have a cooked vegetable? No, you can always substitute 1 cup of raw vegetables for cooked, which would give 2 cups of raw vegetables for that meal.

When I eat out, how can I tell if the salad dressing is sugar-free? When in doubt, use plain oil and vinegar. If you dine in a particular restaurant frequently, ask the waitress to bring you the label of your favorite salad dressing. You would know without asking that Thousand Island and French Dressing would have a high amount of sugar.

Is vegetable "pasta" acceptable on the food plan? No. On most of those products, the first ingredient is either semolina or durum, which are types of wheat. Tiny amounts of vegetables are used in these pastas and noodles for coloring. The vegetables are not major ingredients.

I buy prepared meat at the deli. How can I tell if it is sugar-free? Ask the clerk to read the label to you. Be sure there is NO sugar listed in the ingredients. Remember, we aim for zero sugar on the food plan.

What shall I do at work during coffee break? Plan to have decaf coffee or herb tea and keep a supply of dry milk so that you will not be tempted to use nondairy creamer, which has a high sugar content.

I am hypoglycemic. Is this food plan appropriate for me? Everyone planning to use this food plan should check with their physician before doing so. Since you are under a doctor's care for hypoglycemia, it is especially important for you to take a copy of this food plan to your doctor. Both hypoglycemics and diabetics have found this program helpful in the past, but your doctor may wish to make some adjustments in it. It is possible to divide the food portions into six small meals rather than four without increasing the amount of food.

What happens if I'm sick and can't eat? Stick to your food plan to the best of your ability. Check all your medications to be certain that they are sugar-free. Above all, don't start using the old food remedies such as milk toast, tea and toast and so on. Sick or well, we stay abstinent, one day at a time.

It seems like I'm giving up most of my favorite foods! Give the food plan a chance. Most of our favorite foods are high fat, high carbohydrate. We become so dependent on them that we gradually eliminate many nutritious things from our daily food intake. I suspect you will begin to enjoy many things on the food plan and begin to count them among your favorite foods.

Is it okay to leave some food if I'm not hungry? Weigh, measure and eat it all. There are a number of reasons why this approach is effective. First of all, eating less than the plan calls for constitutes going on a diet. Second, it is important to learn to trust the food plan to fulfill nutritional needs, to lose the craving and to avoid hunger. Also eating too little sets up the next binge. In addition, it is important to maintain the balance between protein and carbohydrate foods. The slogan is: *Food Plan — no more, no less!*

I frequently eat at the homes of family and friends. This concerns me. What can I do to ensure my abstinence? Call before the date when you will eat at another's home. Check the menu and describe your abstinence from sugar, flour and wheat. Take a dish to pass of any food you may need to supplement the menu. Recently I attended an outdoor barbecue where there were more than a hundred guests. Not only was the menu inappropriate, but the meal was served at 2 p.m., which was not good timing for my lunch. I ate before I left home. I joined guests at picnic tables and enjoyed conversation and sugar-free drinks. If your abstinence is threatened at an emotional level by social occasions, stay home. **There are people who encourage me to eat sweet, starchy desserts. What can I do about this?** Avoid being around such people. Abstinence is a matter of life and death for food addicts. While we are in the disease, we seek out others who eat the way we eat. In recovery we must surround ourselves with abstinent people. **Help! I can't cook.** Here is a list of things you might do to make your abstinent meal preparation easier:

- Use one-half cup cottage cheese for protein. It needs no preparation and is good on a baked potato.
- Wash and bake a potato for 5 to 6 minutes on High in a microwave.
- Buy baked deli chicken.
- Use canned kidney beans (protein) and mix with 2 cups of raw vegetables and dressing for a simple salad that is a complete lunch.
- Follow package directions on frozen products such as fish and vegetables.
- Learn to use a microwave.
- Buy prepared raw vegetables at the salad bar.
- Eat predominantly raw fruit and vegetables.
- Mix canned tuna with salad vegetables and the appropriate dressing for Tuna Caesar Salad or Tuna Cole Slaw for one-dish lunches.
- Cook eggs gently over low heat.
- Learn to prepare new dishes when you have ample time to experiment.
- Learn to cook one new dish per week.
- Keep it simple!

Does it matter if I eat fast? Eating fast is a symptom of the disease, that is, the gorging behavior. The faster I eat, the more I can consume. Make a conscious effort to slow down by placing your eating utensil on the plate between each bite. Chew and taste the food to gain greater satisfaction from each meal. If you catch yourself gorging, take an attitude check. Are you allowing yourself to get too hungry, angry, pressured or stressed?

Now that I'm weighing my food every day, how often do I get to weigh me? Good question! You've got the right idea. We stop weighing ourselves and start weighing our food instead. When I was still in the disease of food addiction and dieting, I would weigh myself 10 to 20 times a day — indicating how obsessed with weight I really was. In recovery, we weigh once a month and then once a week when we begin the maintenance food plan. If weighing triggers the obsession with weight for you, discard your scales, abstain from weighing and trust the food plan to work for you.

Initiating Recovery

$\mathcal{T}$his book describes an approach to physical abstinence. It suggests that the basic foundation of recovery is abstaining on a physical level from all mood-altering substances. For the food-addicted individual, abstinence from highly refined foods and all other mood-altering chemicals constitutes not only the beginning of recovery, but the absolute foundation of recovery from food addiction. It is crucial to begin at that point. We take the first step of recovery when we admit that we are powerless over food and that because we are powerless over food, our lives are unmanageable. Understand that this is only the beginning.

No one would be satisfied to build only the foundation of a house and live there forever, nor would any food addict be satisfied to use the food plan and fail to grow

beyond the degree of recovery which the food plan provides. That is what we achieved on some of our diets. It's
not enough. In fact, never to grow beyond physical abstinence isn't recovery at all.

The food plan is provided as a guideline to physical
abstinence only. Because it is complicated and confusing
for food addicts to facilitate abstinence, this plan is offered
as a guide. In order to provide the greatest growth, the
food plan will be accompanied by major changes in the
emotional and spiritual aspects of life. To effect these
changes there are 11 more steps of recovery against which
emotional and spiritual growth can be measured.

This book was written to suggest a way to begin. With
these ideas in mind, it is imperative to seek support in
ongoing recovery. Going it alone is foolhardy. After all,
isn't that what addicts have always done? Most addicts
stand at some time at that turning point of complete
commitment to the disease or complete commitment to
recovery — the moment of truth.

Dee remembers:

> On March 10, 1984, I was sitting at a bar drinking a glass
> of wine, waiting for my table to be called. It was the height
> of the tourist season; restaurants were crowded. I was plan-
> ning to eat dinner in exactly the same style I had done for the
> past 25 years — hard, fast and in such quantities that most
> people would have been humiliated. Not I. Drugged out on
> food and oblivious to stares, I would make trips to the ladies
> room to purge. As I waited, the smells of the bar began to
> annoy me. The people looked sad and frozen in hopelessness.
> I walked out. God had a different plan for me. I'd had
> enough. My time had come to love me, to receive recovery.

Dee's recovery began in a treatment program. For many
others it begins in a meeting of a self-help program such
as Overeaters Anonymous or Food Addicts Anonymous.
Wherever we start, the process is the same. We begin by
taking directions from those who came before us.

What Constitutes Good Treatment?

Good treatment programs meet the following criteria:

1. The first goal of treatment is to break the binge cycle, support the patient through withdrawal and introduce the concept of abstinence from binge foods and other mood-altering chemicals.
2. Next the patient is provided accurate information about the disease of food addiction and understands and accepts that it is a disease — chronic, progressive and fatal in nature.
3. The patient identifies how food addiction has affected his life and the lives of his loved ones.
4. Patients are oriented to the recovery support programs and develop an ongoing support system.
5. Finally patients begin the process of healing and change that will ensure continuing recovery.

What Is Overeaters Anonymous?

Overeaters Anonymous is a fellowship of people whose eating is out of control. OA considers compulsive overeating to be a progressive illness, which cannot be cured but which can be arrested. The OA recovery program is based on the 12 Steps and 12 Traditions of Alcoholics Anonymous. The international address of Overeaters Anonymous is:

**Overeaters Anonymous
World Service Office
4025 Spencer St., #203
Torrance, CA 90503
Phone: (213) 542-8363**

What Is Food Addicts Anonymous?

Food Addicts Anonymous is a fellowship of men and women who are willing to recover from the disease of food addiction. Sharing experience, strength and hope with each other allows members to recover from this disease one day at a time. Food Addicts Anonymous is self-supporting through members' contributions. FAA is not affiliated with any diet or weight loss programs, treatment facilities or religious organizations. FAA neither endorses nor opposes any causes. Their primary purpose is to stay abstinent and help other food addicts achieve abstinence. The international address of Food Addicts Anonymous is:

Food Addicts Anonymous
4623 Forest Hill Blvd., Suite 111-4
West Palm Beach, FL 33415
Phone: (407) 967-3871

How many meetings should I attend? There is no magic number of meetings that will meet the needs of all recovering people. Commitment to recovery and regular attendance at meetings will bring good results. Many people attend 90 meetings in 90 days. Early in recovery such devotion to meetings is a good idea. But it is a bad idea to go to 90/90 and then quit altogether. Follow the guidance of your sponsor or counselor in planning your meeting schedule.

What's a sponsor? A sponsor is someone who will be available to guide you in planning and implementing abstinent meals and the 12 Steps of recovery. Planning meals and reporting them to a sponsor helps a beginner become familiar with the food plan. Sponsorship also provides support and encouragement. Honesty is crucial in this relationship. It is especially important to be honest about food. It is painful to report mistakes or relapses, but it is important to trust and rely on the guidance of a sponsor.

Choosing a sponsor is one of the most critical decisions a newcomer to recovery makes. Look for someone to whom you can talk comfortably and whose program you admire. In selecting a sponsor, ask yourself this question: *Do I want the kind of program she has?* Using the sponsor on a daily basis is one of the hallmarks of success in recovery. Finally, a sponsor brings us out of the isolation of the disease. The disease is a *me* process while recovery is a *we* process. Together we stay abstinent.

What if I need more help than a sponsor can give? You may wish to find a counselor experienced in the treatment of addictions, especially if depression and anxiety persist. Also when there is a history of physical or sexual abuse or other serious issues, clinicians experienced in those areas should be sought out.

What about the family? "Not another diet." "Oh, no, not another diet." That may be what family members say when the food addict starts yet another program. Who knows at the outset whether this time the problem will be solved or if this is just another dead-end street.

The family gets carried along with the food addict in the stream of unhappy events that constitutes food addiction. "How many times will our food plan be changed?" the family wails. "How many times do we have to clean out the cupboard? We've tried seaweed and twig tea, tiny servings of this, huge servings of that, only to turn around and find that we're back on pizza and cake." Or, "What happened to the famous diet you were obsessed with last week? What will you tell us next?"

Certainly the family has suffered along with the addict during the progression of food addiction. The family is involved in their own downward progression, confused and feeling helpless, often angry and resentful, too. In many cases, family members have spent a lot of time and effort cooperating, controlling and criticizing the food addict.

It is usually a surprise to everyone that this is about more than food and diets. The whole family has become involved in the process of a disease called food addiction. It's a relief, too, to realize that since it is a disease no one is at fault.

During the time it takes to "make" a food addict, everyone and everything has been blamed for the problem. Family members may have heard, "I was cross because of you — I ate because of you — I blew my diet because of you." Blame flowed in both directions. The food addict has been blamed for many ills of family life. Cruel words have been exchanged, possibly even blows. No one realized that they were dealing with a chronic illness and many unpleasant side effects. This disease involves the whole family. Each family member was hurt by the disease in body, mind and spirit. Each family member deserves a plan for recovery.

Everyone affected needs to know that the disease of food addiction cannot be cured, but it can be arrested and the damage healed. The positive progression of recovery will work for everyone. Each person can experience recovery at his own rate depending on the amount of effort invested. Recovery is separate and individual. His recovery does not depend on her nor does her recovery depend on him. Some family members may choose to stay sick while others choose health. Obviously, an atmosphere of cooperation and mutual recovery is the ideal situation.

If recovery is chosen, the addict and family members alike must change both attitudes and behavior, basically transforming their lives. The responsibility for these changes rests on each individual separately because only we can change ourselves. That's the message of the Serenity Prayer — we have to sort out what we can change and what we must accept. One thing is certain: We can't change the addict nor can we change the nature of the addiction. Can we admit that we are powerless over people, places and things? Will we be able to admit that we are powerless over the addict and the addiction?

It is difficult, if not impossible, to change without help. Family members are encouraged to seek out 12-Step programs and counselors suited to their own needs in order to develop a plan of recovery that will reverse the process of the disease in their lives. All recovery begins with honesty in the form of admitting that we need the help of others to find our way out of addiction's dilemma. "We grow by our willingness to face and rectify errors and convert them into assets." (1) That work cannot be done alone.

Hopefully many of your questions concerning the disease and the food addict's approach to recovery will be answered within the pages of this book. Now the time has come for each family member to seek his or her own

program of healing in order to begin the process of emotional detachment from the addict. Once the whole family's focus was to make the sick person well. Now the
focus shifts to each individual's personal recovery.

What about men? At a recent meeting of food addicts,
Tom complained that all of the current literature on food
addiction addresses the female food addict's issues. Although addiction is not a separate issue for males or
females, we recognize that being part of a minority is a
problem. Men are a minority in the recovery programs,
both the 12-Step programs for food addiction and treatment programs as well. It can be difficult when there are
no other men with whom to identify.

Often dealing with fat is a different issue for men because society looks at overweight men differently. The
social pressure to be thin does not affect a man as much
as a woman. Some men even say that it is good for a man
to be big, that bigness makes them feel macho. This kind
of thinking will keep its victim in the disease, and it needs
to be confronted.

There is also the dangerous attitude that it's "wimpy" to
be on a food plan. Jay said that other men made remarks
when he was weighing and measuring. He thinks that
dealing with food is considered to be slightly effeminate.

Most men find it difficult to deal with emotions because that's considered wimpy also. "When we were little
boys, the others beat you up if you were a crybaby," says
Fred, who went to treatment for food addiction. He goes
on to say, "I flunked Crying in rehab. I just couldn't do it,
but it's hard to recover when you are unable to reverse
years of being shut down emotionally and unable to
release pain through tears." He adds, "Now I introduce
myself at recovery meetings as a food addict — and it still
feels wimpy to me. Sometimes I think others are judging
me. The other guys are tough drug addict types and I'm
a chocoholic."

With issues such as these, men require mutual support.
The greatest way to gain that support is to work actively
in the program with other men. By carrying the message

to the man who suffers from food addiction, eventually the numbers of recovering men will increase. Also you may wish to develop contacts with other men through the World Service Office of Overeaters Anonymous, as well as at conferences, retreats and conventions.

Whatever the problems that confront men in recovery programs, they are not insurmountable and they cannot be made into excuses to leave recovery and binge again. There is no problem so great that one bite won't make it worse. We encourage all men to apply the 12 Steps of recovery to their lives.

Is there anything that will get me in trouble in recovery? When we get into recovery, we notice certain patterns that may prove to be detrimental. Our goal in recovery is to establish a pattern of sane eating based on an abstinent food plan. There are some patterns that deviate from our commitment to that plan.

Obsessing about food is a dangerous practice which will quickly lead us back into the physical addiction. Recovery happens when we plan, report and implement a simple food plan and then let go of the food, asking God's help and the help of others in our recovery program. We have the power to control our own thoughts, so that, at the mental level, we can substitute healthy recovery thoughts for the destructive thoughts about binge food. Don't forget the disease is operating at the survival level. It takes the combined force of prayer and our helping network to lead us out. Prayers and phone calls can help dispel the thoughts of food from our minds. It is at this level that the battle against the disease of food addiction is won.

Compulsive eating (eating with a vengeance) is usually associated with distress. It is typified by rapid eating of large amounts of the acceptable kinds of food. Compulsive eating is the return to the rapid consumption of a large amount of food in a discrete period of time and could be described as gobbling, cramming, jamming down lots of food — not gentle eating! When this kind of eating happens, it is time for an inventory. There is too much stress, distress, pressure or tension that needs to be resolved.

Overeating may be a gradual process of eating more than the food plan calls for. It usually involves a gradual increase in the amount of food consumed, for instance, eating three-egg omelets when the food plan calls for two eggs or eating 8-ounce steaks on a regular basis. This process chips away at recovery. The day may come when the overeater may no longer be on any food plan because he no longer attends to amounts.

Addictive eating involves returning to sugar, flour, wheat products and food with high-fat content. This kind of relapse means that abstinence is lost, recovery is lost. Addictive eating is a return to the disease. The first bite of those foods triggers the disease which will then begin to operate at the physiological level despite all the mental gymnastics we may perform. Once the disease is triggered, the deadly progression will begin to operate.

There are other dangerous patterns too, such as obsession with weight. Weight loss is not a goal of recovery, it is an outcome. Obsessive thoughts about weight can become a mind set. The number on the scale is not magic. When one becomes obsessed with weight, the mind goes reeling off on its own tangents. When a food addict succumbs to internal or external pressure to be thin, many old destructive ways may be implemented. Remember — thin is not well. Thinness is not the hallmark of recovery. Although weight loss may be associated with recovery, it is not the sum total of recovery. Realistic body weight and realistic weight losses must become part of a saner way of life.

What are the things I should avoid? Don't believe the big lie that one bite will satisfy the craving. Not only will it *not* satisfy the craving, it will constitute a commitment to the craving, guaranteeing that it will endure.

No matter what happens in the course of recovery, no matter how bad life might be, the highest priority in recovery is avoiding relapse and the only way to avoid relapse is to keep from taking that first compulsive bite of binge food. As long as the disease is no longer triggered at the physical level, there is a chance to work out living problems. Remember, problems don't cause addiction, addiction causes problems.

In order to stay in recovery, catch yourself in the act of behaving in ways which might threaten abstinence. Be vigilant and stay aware of dangerous attitudes and behaviors.

Avoid food products that you are not sure about. Remember, when in doubt, leave it out.

Avoid setting goals that are related to weight loss. Make recovery your number one priority and let weight loss take care of itself. Weight loss happens while you are doing something else.

Don't take the first bite of binge food. Abstain from that first bite for a minute, for an hour, for a day. String together days of abstinence for a lifetime of recovery.

Don't stay trapped in the addiction, ask for help. Everyone who has ever escaped addiction has done it by the grace of God and the helping hand of a recovering food addict.

Food addiction is a lonely disease. It breeds in isolation. Beware of being alone too much. Get a sponsor who will work with you on the food plan and the 12 Steps. At meetings, get phone numbers of people to call when the going gets tough. You don't have to be alone anymore.

Keep your mind open to all new information and concepts. Dannie, a former patient, related that while in treatment she began doubting the validity of this approach. She says, "What changed my course of resistance was a simple statement by my therapist: 'It's okay if you don't believe. Just trust that *we* believe.' " Dannie goes on to say, "I was the product of all my own best efforts and thoughts. Unfortunately at that point, all of my best had stopped working. It was time to trust my therapist's program because hers was working just fine!"

Pride can keep you in the disease. Remember, it is necessary to ask for help to escape this powerful disease. Everyone who has gone before you has reached out for the help of a stronger person.

Don't give up before you start. Give yourself a chance. Try this program of recovery for 90 days, then evaluate the results. I am convinced that life will be better. Don't let impulse rule your life. Think! Think! Think! In recovery we must start thinking before acting. An impulsive act of eating can put us back into the disease and all the horror that goes with it.

Don't fall for the lie that one bite of binge food will satisfy.

Avoid focusing on what you don't have. Think about what you do have. Make a gratitude list. Count the rewards of recovery rather than the sacrifices you've had to make. Remember you are dealing with a disease. Would you rather have another one? The prescription for recovery from this illness involves eating sensibly. That's what reasonable people have been doing all along.

Stop trusting your own resources. Willpower doesn't work. Recovery groups offer experience, strength and hope. Go there for support and encouragement.

When bad days occur, don't assume the problem is emotional. Always look to the physical first. Have you eaten anything that might trigger the disease? Beware of artificial sweeteners, hidden sugar and other forms of sweetener such as fruit juices. You are sensitive to them. Are you hungry, angry, lonely, tired or physically ill? Check the food you have eaten for hidden wheat. Are you eating all of the food called for in the food plan or are you cutting back, leaving yourself undernourished?

Be prepared for physical withdrawal to create discomfort on both the physical and emotional levels. You may experience symptoms of headache, nausea, body ache, shakiness, depression or lethargy. A long history of toxic eating may result in any or all of these uncomfortable feelings. If discomfort persists beyond ten days, you may wish to consult your doctor. Stay in touch with your sponsor during the period of withdrawal. She will be able to offer support.

Progressive Recovery – Reversing The Disease

Surrender

$\mathcal{R}$ecovery begins with surrender to the fact of the addiction, that is, when we admit that we are powerless over binge food. We are ready to surrender when we realize that food addiction is the way to death and recovery is the way to life. We surrender at that moment of desperation when we know that we can't handle it any longer, when we admit that we have no power over our eating.

Like Andy, who knew with overwhelming certainty that he couldn't take it any more. He said, "I know how the Emperor of Japan felt when he surrendered to the Allied commanders. He must have thought of the destruction and devastation caused by the atomic bomb and said, 'Just stop the bombing.' " Andy went on to say, "That is what I want — just stop bombing me." Somehow, through all of the denial and delusion that kept Andy in the disease, the grace of God touched him so that his eyes were opened and for the first time he could make the connection between his food addiction and his pain.

When the food addict admits and accepts powerlessness over binge food, recovery begins. Admission springs from the lips, acceptance operates at gut level. Acceptance implies that food addiction is a fact of (our) life! Food addiction is our reality. Acceptance may be a long-term process. However long it takes, the addict risks relapse until acceptance happens. While the addict hangs between admission and acceptance, he will live in anger, frustration and pain because he knows the truth, but he will not embrace that truth.

All recovery begins with a call for help. When we hit bottom in the disease, we cry out for help to the God of our understanding. We may not even remember the plea, but it was made. It may have been a prayer so simple that it was one or two simple words, *Help* or *Help me*, whispered or shouted when we were at the depth of despair. Usually the plea is made with no thought that help could ever come.

An Honest Desire For Help

When the suffering food addict, with a desire for help, meets a recovering food addict, hope is born. In my own case, a woman I knew slightly asked, "Have you ever heard about the program for people with food problems?" With those words, she introduced me to a program of recovery which has offered me help and hope since 1977.

Breaking The Binge Cycle

To arrest the disease of food addiction, the food addict must stop eating binge food immediately, completely and permanently. Physical recovery begins when we stop using binge food, fasting, purging, excessive exercise and all the unhealthy methods of weight control. This is accomplished by making a commitment to the abstinent food plan. Since the foundation of all recovery is abstinence from the substance of addiction, recovery requires that the addict complete the withdrawal process. This entails that we endure the discomfort of adjustment to the physical deprivation of the substance.

Withdrawal from refined carbohydrates may result in a variety of physical symptoms varying from mild to intense. Whatever the intensity of the symptoms of withdrawal, it is the discomfort in this early phase of recovery which causes most food addicts to return to binge food because the unpleasant feelings are relieved by eating binge food. Sadly, the relief is short-lived. More and more of the substance is required to maintain a feeling of balance. Avoiding withdrawal in this manner keeps most addicts *in* the disease. Return to binge food is the greatest barrier to recovery.

Withdrawal from refined carbohydrates is complicated for some food addicts by withdrawal from other addictive substances as well, such as alcohol, cocaine, speed or tranquilizers. The list goes on to include all the addictive substances.

Finding Support

For some, the initial phase of recovery is completed in a protected environment under medical supervision. Others find help in recovery programs. The support of other recovering people gives hope and is a crucial element of successful recovery. Going it alone is a bad decision. Support and help are crucial in this endeavor. Life depends on it.

For those who are willing to bear the discomfort of withdrawal and remain abstinent while getting through the pain, the rewards of recovery will be won. Most who take this plan and use it without help and guidance will fail.

Learning That Food Addiction
Is A Treatable Disease

Hope is born when the food addict is provided the correct information about the disease of food addiction. It is a relief to find that food addiction is not caused by our lack of willpower nor is it a mental problem. Rather, it is a primary disease which causes other diseases. It does not originate in the mind, although it does result in mental, emotional and behavioral problems. Likewise, the cause is not spiritual, although addiction creates soul sickness. It is a disease which is the root cause of our problems, not the other way around. Our problems do not cause us to be food addicts. Although a person may have had a bad childhood, the reason she eats compulsively is not that she had a bad childhood, but rather that she has a biogenetic disease.

Because it is a disease, food addiction can be arrested. The newcomer to recovery must understand that there is help and hope. With this understanding, positive thinking begins. During the recovery process the newcomer learns from other recovering people that food addiction is a disease that can be arrested. Food addicts share their experience, strength and hope with each other. Through this process of honest sharing, recovering individuals hold out the offer of progressive recovery to all who might wish to take it. A word of caution: **An individual who is truly addicted cannot claim to be cured.** The addict's biochemistry remains a permanent physical condition. Addiction is a disease which can be arrested by participation in the Anonymous programs, therapy and avoiding relapse into the disease.

Understanding Abstinence Is
The Foundation Of Recovery

Abstinence from binge food (trigger food) works. An honest appraisal shows us that binge foods are the ones we can't stop eating once we start *and* all other food made up of the same ingredients *even if we think we don't like them.* Remember, addiction is not about likes and dislikes. It is operating at the instinctual level of our being. **The body will always know what triggers the addiction. The mind lies.** If we can't handle sugar, flour and fatty foods in one form, we cannot handle them in other forms. Abstinence means one day at a time, not eating binge foods *at all,* and eliminating *all* foods that will trigger the addiction. We can't do it for the rest of our lives but we *can* do it just for today. Abstinence is different because we no longer feel deprived. We begin to see that we got rid of something harmful — the addiction — along with the pain and the sense of failure.

Letting Go Of Obsessions
With Food And Weight

We do not list weight loss among the goals of recovery although it is a reasonable expectation. As weight gain was a symptom of the disease, weight loss is a symptom of recovery. One of the major changes we make in our thinking, when we are no longer practicing dieting mentality, is our attitude about weight. Once we shift into the new attitudes of recovery, we let go of our old ideas. Let go we must or we will be unable to change. We change or die. That is the real choice. If you worry about weight, just sit and watch recovering people looking better and better. Listen to them carefully. They're not talking about weight or diets or food. They are discussing the principles of recovery. Recently a woman asked, "When I lose the weight, will I be able to eat some foods that are not on the food plan which are not a problem for me?" Her recovery is shaky as long as she continues to focus on food and weight. Recovery is freedom from those obsessions and concerns. In recovery, we let go of food one day at a time. Then we are able to turn our attention to the more important matters of life.

A recovering friend named *Sally* shares:

> When I got binge food out of my body, I stopped thinking
> about it. When I'm clean, I don't think about food. I certainly
> thought about it a lot when I was using. Being clean relieves
> me of the obsession. Those relentless thoughts and being
> driven to eat are what addiction is all about.

The use of binge food triggers the use of *more* binge
food. A commonly asked question is, "Do feelings trigger
the use of food?" An uncomfortable feeling can take me
back to food if I decide to eat because of it, but at that point
I have a choice to eat or not. Once I have taken the first
bite of binge food, I have given up the choice because the
addiction has been triggered. At that point, choice is lost,
control is lost and the progression of the disease will begin
again. The progression will not start at the beginning, but
at the stage which I have reached. No problem is so bad
that one bite won't make it worse. Instead of dealing with
one bad feeling, we'll be dealing with a raging addiction.

When I'm clean, I may think about food, but I don't have
to obsess about it because I can control my thoughts. And
I certainly do not have to eat it. I think of this formula:

$D + 1 = C.$ *(Desire plus One bite equals Compulsion)*

Once I take that first bite, I have made the decision to
move back into the compulsive use of binge food. When I
move back into the compulsion, I lose everything.

Diet Mentality Is Replaced By Recovering Attitude

We can stop dieting and start living. We don't have to go
on or off diets anymore. Once we accept the food plan as
a way of life, we can quit shopping for the magic way that
never panned out anyway. We can accept the fact that
there are no quick fixes to this addiction and discontinue
the wishes and the dreams that never came true, depending
instead on a proven way of life and recovering people who
will lead us out of the addiction into a way that works.

Physical And Emotional Health Improves

We no longer have to subject our bodies to inadequate nutrition because the food plan provides good nutrition. We can be grateful for the fresh fruit and vegetables, lean meat, poultry and fish, whole grains and low-fat dairy products provided by the food plan. How much better I feel about those foods than the food I ate the last day I binged. They were all sticky, pasty, greasy foods which nauseated me then as the thought of them nauseates me now. We no longer have to fill our bodies with binge food which depletes our bodies of vitamins and minerals. Now we can put good food in our bodies because we are no longer forced *against our wills* by the addiction to eat binge food. We don't feel hungry because we are adequately nourished. We are no longer being driven by cravings and will be satisfied with the adequate intake of food provided by the food plan.

Once we find recovery, we no longer have to go through the binge-diet or binge-purge cycle again. We can effect a permanent change. We will be able to live a sane and productive life.

In the early stages of recovery, medical help may be required due to the many medical conditions caused by food addiction. The following letter indicates the reaction of one physician to the program.

James R. Shaw, M.D., Addictions Specialist, says:

I am truly amazed at the impact the food plan you have developed has on patients in our controlled milieu. I am writing now because we have just such another case in point. It is so gratifying to see a food plan work when all of my outpatient, family practice experience had made me cynical about hoping to effect such improvements in diabetes, lipid disorders or hypertension.

Our newest patient is a "hopelessly" overweight, adult-onset, insulin-dependent diabetic. Upon admission she was on 100 units of NPH insulin in the morning and 40 units of NPH before supper. It is now four days later and she is already down to 30 units in the morning and 12 units before supper — a 70% decrease in just four days. Another recent patient dropped from 62 units of NPH insulin on admission to 18 units by discharge — a 71% decrease.

One of the most exciting areas of change has been in total cholesterol determination. Part of our routine lab work is to check the patient's cholesterol. Several patients had cholesterol elevated in the 260-280 range. Traditional approaches to hypercholesterolemia dictate dietary management as a first line treatment with the best possible scenario being a 15% reduction in cholesterol to 220-240. Perhaps that is the case in persons eating "normal" amounts of the wrong things but in our bulimics, cholesterol is routinely reduced within three weeks to 60-70% of admission values.

Quite a few of our hypertensive patients have discontinued their antihypertensive medications or have had to change to milder agents. Again, these effects are noted many times within days of admission.

As the food addict moves through the steps of recovery, practicing the principles of recovery, seeking and giving help and learning a new way of life, he begins to experience the benefits of recovery. Often the physical body will respond in an amazingly short time to the food plan. As Dr. Shaw describes, medical conditions have been known to remit in a matter of days or weeks. No matter what the speed of recovery is from medical conditions associated with food addiction, we can expect progress in that area for individuals who make basic changes in their approach to food.

Recovering food addicts begin to experience natural rest and sleep and the feelings of health and heightened energy which result. With this blessing of recovery, we begin to become productive individuals.

Bob entered treatment in a wheelchair. He was suffering from the pain of advanced arthritis. At that time, he was retired from his business because he was no longer able to move about. In recovery he is not only able to work actively in his business, but he is attending college, earning credits which will enhance his knowledge of business, and he is also active in his 12-Step program of recovery. He has been given a whole new life of activity.

As we begin to know peace and serenity, our fears and anxieties begin to diminish. These are the fringe benefits of recovery. Where we used to avoid others and live in agonizing isolation, we begin to seek out and enjoy the company of others. We can assess our many talents and make use of them as we begin to move freely about the world. With all of this, we begin to have good feelings about ourselves, and we experience improved physical health and appearance.

Returning Self-Esteem

We enjoy the progressive return of self-worth. Responsible behavior, good health, freedom from guilt and hopeful thoughts produce a happier individual. Often pride in our appearance is renewed. As we start to feel better about ourselves, we can that now believe we're worth it — a new hairstyle, suit or manicure.

Accepting Life On Life's Terms

Our thinking becomes more realistic when we understand that there is no quick fix or easy way out of the disease of food addiction. We can take our lives off hold and begin to achieve happiness, growth and sanity despite our weight. Once we start heading away from the disease, we can begin to experience life. We don't have to wait until we reach our goal weight to buy nice clothes, dance, go on a cruise, go to college, start a business or take our kids to the park. We are free to be the people we wish to be. We can hold our heads up with the knowledge that we are doing our best today.

The food addict in recovery can begin to accept life on life's terms. Life becomes simpler without the complications of the active addiction. This is not to say that we climb on a cloud of serenity and float there for the duration of our recovery. Although the road will be bumpy, we will be able to seek solutions to the day-to-day complexities of living as long as we remain in recovery. We still have to face the tough situations that all humans deal with — death, divorce, job stress or family problems. In recovery there is help so we can get through without returning to the disease. When times are tough, we reach out to draw on the experience, strength and hope of another recovering person. The love among recovering people is strong because it is the love of one addict for another who shares the experience of suffering.

Recovery is about healing. The healing takes place on all levels of our being — physical, emotional and spiritual. How far can we go? The sky's the limit! Our potential in recovery is unlimited as long as we continue to grow. Without growth there is regression. Going backwards is heading back into the disease.

Relationships Improve

As every aspect of life was affected by the disease of food addiction, so every aspect of life feels the impact of recovery. Family members, co-workers, employers will be affected. Those who were suspicious, frustrated and disgusted by our obsessive-compulsive eating may be skeptical and afraid to trust again, but time is our ally in recovery. Every day is a new beginning. We have nothing to prove to anyone. We string together abstinent days to create an abstinent life. Eventually relationships improve.

Eileen, who is two years into recovery, writes:

> My husband and I have a chance today to have what I always wanted from my very soul, a loving and whole relationship with another person. My relationship with my children is real today. There is trust that never existed before because I am trustworthy. Abstinent, I can mean what I say and say what I mean.

Hope Is Born

We begin to face the future with a more positive attitude. We develop interest in new things and are able to follow through on old interests. It is not unusual for a recovering person to earn a college degree, participate in sports and regular exercise, develop a skill, start a business, write a book or win promotions at work. The world opens up as we begin to partake of life instead of sticky, pasty, greasy food.

What we do with our recovery is up to us. We may emphasize the physical, strive for emotional balance or work toward spiritual growth. The choice is ours.

My friend Jimmy says, "If you keep on doing what you're doing, you'll keep on getting what you're getting!" When we abstain from the first bite of binge food, go to meetings, call our sponsor and read recovery literature, the payoff will be a strong recovery.

Action is the magic of recovery. Contact with others helps us continue to grow in self-understanding and to learn how to *live* this program. Expressing our feelings to others in the program provides an outlet for stress. Regular contact with other food addicts is a reminder of what it was like in the disease, what happened to change that and what it is like now in recovery.

Freedom And Happiness

When we belong to ourselves instead of the refrigerator, we marvel at our new freedom. Where once we were enslaved by binge food, we now begin to enjoy the promises of recovery.

"We are going to know a new freedom and a new happiness. We will not regret the past nor wish to shut the door on it. We will comprehend the word serenity and we will know peace. No matter how far down the scale we have gone, we will see how our experience can benefit others. That feeling of uselessness and self-pity will slip away. Our whole attitude and outlook upon life will change. Fear of people and of economic insecurity will leave us. We will intuitively know how to handle situations which used to baffle us. We will suddenly realize that God is doing for us what we could not do for ourselves.

"Are these extravagant promises? We think not. They are being fulfilled among us. They will always materialize if we work for them." (1)

The work of recovery begins when we start to hear the message our body sends: We are powerless over addictive foods. In recovery we finally begin to comprehend what our body already knows.

Food Addiction
Relapse Prevention

Due to the destructive nature of the disease of food addiction and the complications related to maintaining long-term recovery, there are those who experience relapse. Recently Jill, who was in relapse, told us: "My world got narrower and narrower — fewer clothes, fewer food choices, fewer friends and fewer things to do." Jill, who was so animated in recovery, became incapacitated in relapse. She returned to binge eating despite the negative consequences.

People who relapse have a history of attempts to recover from food addiction without lasting success. They resume binge or binge-purge behavior despite involvement in a recovery program. Relapse-prone individuals continue to obsess about food, weight and body image.

For those who relapse, the recovery process is affected by the inability to think clearly, memory problems, emotional outbursts, depression, continued anxiety, sleep disturbances and hypersensitivity to stress.

Understanding Relapse

Relapse does not begin with the first bite of binge food. It is a spontaneous, often unconscious, process which ends with binge eating. The key to continued recovery is to be aware of this process in order to guard against it in the earliest stages possible. Most food addicts relapse because they do not know how to stop the process, nor do they recognize the process while it is occurring. Relapse involves the performance of increasingly more disease-related tasks while performing fewer recovery-related ones. Relapse is like walking backward toward the disease, discarding recovery tools along the way. Relapse occurs in the absence of strong active recovery efforts. The process is complete when the individual becomes so dysfunctional in recovery that she returns to the use of the addictive substance. At that time the disease is triggered at the physical level and the relapse process ends. "Relapse is the process where your thoughts, feelings and actions get so out of control that you use . . . to feel better." (1)

Relapse begins with isolated self-defeating behaviors which, if left unchecked, develop into destructive patterns. Avoiding relapse for those in early stage recovery involves recognizing the threats to developing stable recovery before they have become habitual. Jill says, "I know how to get abstinent, I pray to learn how to keep it." The key to Jill's recovery is that she learn to recognize her personal danger signs of relapse and develop a way to manage dangerous attitudes and behaviors.

Maintaining Abstinence

An inventory of one's relationship with food can give clues to the quality of recovery and the risk of relapse. The relapse process, in general, will look something like the following diagram, starting with good clean abstinence. The movement is downward through problem eating toward addictive eating, which involves the return to the addictive substances.

> Clean Abstinence
> Overeating
> Undereating
> Compulsive eating
> Addictive eating

Clean abstinence involves compliance with a food plan by weighing and measuring, planning and scheduling meals, selecting a variety of safe foods, reading labels and, in general, feeling good about the approach to food and food choices. This is where we like to be.

Overeating involves increasing the volume of some or all foods by design or a casual approach to food management. Remember, this is part of the relapse process, not the whole process. By the way, one extra green bean *does not* constitute a relapse. Jill says, "I remember people saying, 'Because I ate an extra green bean, I figured I blew it, so I went out and ate it all.' " An extra bean would have no effect on recovery but that kind of irrational thinking can destroy us. However, when we rationalize genuine overeating, we are in the relapse *process.*

Undereating often signals a return to weight consciousness and the diet mentality. Some might choose only low calorie foods and eliminate high calorie ones altogether. Some of the most common errors that lead to relapse include skipping the evening dairy and fruit portions, cutting out the fat portion and reducing the protein serving. Skipping meals or skipping portions is a setup to be hungry and obsessed with food. Undereating is taking the fast track through the relapse process back into the disease.

Compulsive eating usually signals that food is being used to deal with feelings. A behavior is compulsive when it is used to cope with pain. Jill remembers returning from work in the evening feeling frustrated and angry upon finding her 14-year-old son in a messy living room. She quickly fixed her dinner and ate it rapidly to soothe her feelings. Although the meal was an abstinent one, she didn't feel good about the way she ate it. Jill related that it was hard to stop eating after that episode and she had to fight a binge that evening. She tells about a similar incident when she got angry at work just before dinner and chomped on her food, postponing dealing with her feelings.

Addictive eating is crossing the line that separates recovery from addiction. It is at this point that the relapse process ends and the disease begins. When a food addict crosses that line, she will no longer be able to predict when or if she will be able to stop eating addictively.

Addictive eating is triggered by the use of addictive foods. We have learned from patients in relapse treatment that the return to addictive eating preceded the return to the use of other addictive substances as well. In other words, once the process begins, we cannot predict which substances we will take back, including drugs, alcohol and nicotine. For many, eating trigger food occurs not as a conscious choice but due to failure to check ingredients or not understanding exactly which foods actually trigger food addiction.

The relapse process entails moving back and forth between good clean abstinence and total relapse which involves the use of addictive foods. "Relapse and recovery are intimately related. You cannot experience recovery from addiction without experiencing a tendency toward relapse. Relapse tendencies are a normal and natural part of the recovery process." (2)

Clean Abstinence	Recovery
Overeating	
Undereating	Relapse Process
Compulsive eating	
Addictive eating	Disease

The good news is that we can stop the process before we cross the line into the addictive use of binge food — before we return to the full blown disease — by recognizing the warnings.

Danger Signs

Sloppy measurements

Increase in volume

Decrease in the frequency of measuring

Negotiating with the food plan

Skipping meals

Eating between meals

Reducing portion size for weight loss

Setting unrealistic weight-loss goals

Increasing amounts of high carbohydrate foods

Neglecting to check lists of ingredients for trigger substances

Binging on abstinent food, including high carbohydrate foods, proteins and fats

Discontinuing the scheduling of meals

Eating while distracted by TV, newspaper, kids

Stopping the planning, recording, reporting, committing and letting go of food

Failing to report changes in the food plan

Returning to obsession with food and weight

Returning to dieting, fasting and/or purging

Adding trigger foods, such as bananas, raisins, nuts and chocolate in the form of "diet" candy and "diet" desserts

Eating wheat and flour

Eating sugar

Using other addictive substances, such as nicotine, caffeine, alcohol or pot

Abstinence is the beginning and the foundation of recovery. Yet there is much more to accomplish in order to
keep the gift of recovery. Recovery is based on work in
many areas.

Post-Acute Withdrawal Threatens Recovery

Dr. G. Bell, working with alcoholics in Toronto, Canada,
since 1946, developed a model of recovery which illustrat-
ed movement in recovery from the state of disease to a
state of unease and finally to a state of ease. This model
is realistic. It shows that recovery starts while the individual is still deep in the disease. It takes time and effort
to move out of the disease state through the stage of
unease to a state of ease. Addictive substances damage
the body, mind and spirit. Discomfort is experienced as
the body and brain adjust to life without chemicals, starting with withdrawal and continuing through the Post-
Acute Withdrawal (PAW). Recovering people need to understand that putting down the substance does not guar-
antee that they will climb onto a pink cloud of serenity
and float happily along. Life without substances includes
varying degrees of withdrawal and post-acute withdrawal
symptoms. Terence T. Gorski, who has researched the
PAW model says, "Post-acute withdrawal symptoms are
not the same in everyone. They vary in how severe they
are, how often they occur and how long they last." (3) He
has identified the types of PAW Symptoms as follows:

1. Inability to think clearly
2. Memory problems
3. Emotional over-reactions or numbness
4. Sleep disturbances
5. Physical coordination problems
6. Stress sensitivity (4)

Understanding that these kinds of symptoms will occur
and devising strategies to manage them aid in formulating
a strong and realistic program of recovery. Recovery and
therapy groups will lend support to the newly recovering

person through the discomfort of PAW. A proactive approach including learning stress management, physical exercise, journaling, meditation, breathing exercises, yoga and other healthful practices can aid one in dealing with post-acute withdrawal symptoms.

Emotional Threats To Recovery

When addicts withdraw from the substances of addiction, feelings surface. Since food addicts have used food as a drug to kill feelings, this puts the newly recovered person in a difficult situation without the mood-altering substance or the skills to deal with the pain. Repressed rage, shame, anxiety and depression will rise during early recovery. A powerful temptation to relapse results from the desire to eat because of these strong feelings.

Learning to identify, express and experience feelings is an early task of recovery which aids in avoiding relapse. An addict's style of dealing with feelings would be to "eat because of them." A person new to recovery doesn't know what to call feelings or what to do about them. New patterns of dealing with emotions will emerge. Some of these patterns will be effective. Other patterns will be ineffective. In order to develop helpful methods of expressing feelings, it is a good idea to enlist the aid of a therapist who will provide guidance in effective ways of dealing with emotional pain.

Some ineffective styles of expressing feelings include blame, criticism, angry outbursts, silence, repression and denial resulting in grandiosity, perfectionism, impulsiveness, obsessions and compulsions, self-pity and victimhood. The consequences of avoiding dealing with feelings are increased negative feelings, negative effect on relationships, decreased self-esteem, physical symptoms and inability to resolve life issues.

An effective means of managing emotions is to name them, claim them and dump them. This is certainly more easily said than done, but the idea is to identify feelings, take responsibility for them and to talk about them with a sponsor, therapist or other recovery support person.

The next step is to express these feelings to the person directly involved. Getting past the fear and vulnerability of experiencing and expressing emotions is an early and humbling chore of recovery. Jill said that the first time she decided to take a chance and talk about her feelings was with a grocery clerk in a store she visited infrequently. This seemed like a safe place to her. She was surprised when the clerk failed to react at all when she mentioned a feeling. Jill didn't start talking about feelings with the major players in her life. She started small, practiced a lot and worked her way up to more significant people and feelings.

A daily inventory will aid in identifying the feelings of the day which require attention. Honesty about feelings is a powerful tool to prevent relapse. I strongly support the position that newly recovering people avoid opening painful issues from the past too early in recovery. This includes family-of-origin and abuse issues. Stay in the here-and-now while you develop a strong base in recovery.

Some Danger Signs

Hostility toward people and circumstances
Anger when certain subjects are discussed
Aggravation with authority figures
Irritation when criticized
Frustrated when things don't go my way
Demanding things be done my way
Frequent bouts of depression
Resenting people, places and things
Bad things happen only to me (self-pity)
Feeling insecure about measuring up to others
Showing intolerance by cutting others down
Impatience with others, traffic, waiting in line
Jealousy over what others have and do
Sadness, wanting to give up on life
Feelings of worthlessness and inappropriate guilt
Anxiety and panic attacks
Nameless fears

Mental Mismanagement Threatens Recovery

Dishonesty

The mind lies — only the mind can lie. Denial, delusion, deceit and dishonesty are part of the disease process. Yet honesty, openness and willingness are critical components of recovery. A lifetime of lies and deceit cannot be allowed to persist in recovery. The Big Lie can take us back into the disease: "You can safely eat anything you want" or "Just a little won't hurt." This kind of thinking is overcome through the use of prayer, group therapy, 12-Step meetings, the inventory steps and frequent contact with a sponsor.

Negative Thoughts

Since food addiction is a negative process with nasty consequences, it is not surprising that the addict's perceptions become negative during the course of the disease. If negative and illogical thinking persists, depression and anxiety will continue as well. Pessimistic thoughts will trigger bad feelings and self-defeating behaviors. Our thoughts create our world. Gloomy thoughts create a gloomy world: "I never do anything right" or "I'll just stay in bed. Nothing is going to go right anyway." Addicts need Attitude Adjustments. Close contact with a sponsor, regular attendance at meetings and group therapy provide association with people who will challenge self-defeating ideas. Affirmations and rational responses are tools that can be learned to change negative thoughts and irrational ideas. Self-defeating thought patterns can be challenged and changed in group and individual therapy sessions.

Obsession

Obsession is like entertaining a mental whirlwind of thoughts about food. In obsession it seems as if everything is out of control. Obsessions constitute a serious threat to recovery. Sometimes thoughts of food take over when they are least expected. The good news is that we can control our thoughts; they do not control us. Since we can only think about one thing at a time, the Serenity Prayer can be used like a faucet to shut off unwanted preoccupation with food.

> God grant me the serenity
> To accept the things I cannot change,
> Courage to change the things I can
> And the wisdom to know the difference.

Euphoric Recall

Remembering all of the good times and tastes and forgetting the guilt, vomit and rapid weight gains is typical of euphoric recall. Selective memory causes addicts to remember all of the fond memories while excluding the negative truths about binge eating. A review of the powerlessness and unmanageability of life in the disease can aid in dispelling the irrational ideas that binge food resulted in good feelings. No matter what, food addiction is the commitment to short-term pleasure and long-term pain.

Awfulizing Abstinence

"We look at our perception of abstinence. We say look at how awful and terrible it is. How do we do that? Well, we focus on every little negative in our current abstinence and we blow it all out of proportion and we block out all of the good stuff. We totally eliminate all of the good stuff." (5) Just as food addicts may fondly remember the good old days of gorging, so, too, may they think less than fondly about maintaining recovery. "Is this all there is?" or "It isn't worth it" or "I just wasn't cut out to handle life on life's terms." With this kind of thinking, the next binge seems like a better idea than all the work that recovery requires.

Make a list of the ways that you convince yourself that abstinence is awful and the disease is preferable. Discuss these things with your sponsor and other support people in order to avoid acting upon irrational ideas.

Challenge each mistaken thought with a positive argument *for* recovery.

How To Deal With Irrational Ideas

Terry Gorski formulated the following questions designed to challenge irrational ideas. (6)

1. How do I defend my right to eat binge food?
   Challenge _____
2. How do I convince myself that I am an exception to the rule?
   Challenge _____
3. What are my favorable food-related memories?
   Challenge _____
4. How do I convince myself that maintaining a food plan is awful and terrible?
   Challenge _____
5. How do I convince myself that food will fix me?
   Challenge _____

Lack Of Power Threatens Recovery

"Lack of power, that was our dilemma. We had to find a power by which we could live, and it had to be a Power greater than ourselves." (7) As the disease of food addiction took over, it blocked all healthy relationships with God and man. It is by learning, practicing and incorporating the recovery principles into our lives that we begin to grow spiritually. Remember, recovery means progress: going forward, building, learning and healthy change. Through the practice of daily spiritual assignments, we become part of something greater than ourselves.

While in the disease, food addicts place faith and trust in food, which becomes the major source of security. Turning to it in good times and in bad, it becomes a god. This god never gives, it only takes away. In recovery we must find a greater source of power. The book *Alcoholics Anonymous* says, ". . . that One is God. May you find Him now." (8) Addicts find that Power living the 12 Steps.

The Twelve Steps: A Spiritual Way Of Life

Without a program of recovery, the food plan is just a diet and diets don't work. Maintaining a proactive program is crucial to maintaining abstinent recovery. A saying around the meeting rooms is "The same behavior brings the same results."

Jill claims, "If I keep on attending meetings, working the 12 Steps, calling my sponsor and following directions, the results are pretty good. I can get to school every day and manage my responsibilities. When I stop, everything falls apart. I start to prioritize school instead of recovery, and I lose everything — especially school. It is one of the paradoxes of recovery: Whatever I put before recovery, I lose!"

When recovering food addicts attend fewer meetings, seek out other recovering people less frequently and allow recovery literature to collect dust, relapse is in progress. Consistent attendance at meetings, a viable relationship with a sponsor and continued practice and study of the recovery principles give consistent results.

Jill realized that she was isolating when the answering machine was taking most of her calls, she began missing meetings, called her sponsor only occasionally and stayed in her room most nights. Being home alone away from her support system created the perfect opportunity for overeating, then binge eating and finally addictive eating.

More Relapse Warning Signs

- Decreases attendance at 12-Step recovery meetings
- Stops practice of the recovery principles
- Withdraws from sponsor and other active members of recovery programs
- Ceases performing inventory work
- Discontinues reading recovery literature and listening to recovery tapes
- Neglects prayer and meditation practices
- Begins to question if food addiction really is the problem

Remember that each recovering person is in charge of his own process. Collect all of the tools you can find, enlist all of the helpful people you can identify to aid in the cause of your recovery and, above all, invite God in to help.

Marianne's Story

At the age of 13, I had my first binge and purge. Within one year I was binging every day. In three years it increased to three times a day and by the sixth year I was binging and purging eight times a day. At that point, I was stealing money and food to get my fix and throwing up behind trees in the woods and into garbage bags in my closet. I knew I had a problem but no matter what I tried, I couldn't stop. I went to psychologists, psychiatrists, school counselors, teachers, dietitians, medical doctors, family friends, self-help groups and even priests to get help. No one could help me.

After seven years I finally ended up in a hospital in a food addiction unit. I was out of control. I had hit my bottom. Feeling desperate, I was willing to do anything to get better. I was given *Food Addiction: The Body Knows* and was astounded that someone wrote a book about me who didn't even know me at all. I was immediately convinced about the philosophy of food addiction and knew that I was a food addict. I felt grateful that there is a way to live in recovery.

It took me almost two years to get into recovery. Although I knew that being sugar-, wheat- and flour-free, weighing and measuring my food, going to 12-Step recovery meetings for food addicts and working 12-Step recovery was what I needed to stay in recovery, I thought I could do it my way instead and be successful. I was wrong. The day came when I began binging and purging again. Within one day I was back to vomiting eight times in a 24-hour time period. This time I was vomiting blood.

I knew that if I didn't get more help, I would surely die soon. It wasn't long after that I was back in the hospital on a new unit. This unit was called the Relapse Recovery Unit. It was here that I learned where relapse begins. I didn't know that relapse starts long before I take a bite of addictive food. I learned that relapse starts when my feelings and thoughts get out of control and I don't acknowledge that I have a problem. If I don't deal with my problems, my life will go out of control and I will inevitably overeat. Once I eat addictive food, I am no longer in the relapse process — I am in my disease.

I tried to be perfect with my food plan and my best efforts landed me back in the hospital. I finally realized that I needed to let God into my life to help me. I believed in God and loved Him very much, but I saw that I never actually let Him inside me to take over. Once I did, I felt scales fall from my eyes and weights lift off my shoulders. Best of all, I felt a new joy in my heart. I realized that all God wanted from me was to follow the program and stick close to Him. He would do the rest. It was so simple I could barely comprehend it.

Today I am 22, living in recovery. I know that today is mine. My disease is in remission for now. It is vital for me to live an honest life. My recovery depends on it. If I have a feeling, I express it. If I have a problem, I find a way to deal with it. If I don't deal with my situation, I know I will end up back in my disease. One thing I see clearly is that if I stay abstinent, work the 12 Steps of recovery and stick close to God, He will provide me with a life far more wonderful than I could ever have imagined.

Appendix I

Quick Reference Food Plan

Consult your physician before using this or any other food plan.

ABSTAIN FROM ALL FORMS OF: Alcohol, cocoa, chocolate, "sugar-free" candy, "sugar-free" pudding, "sugar-free" frozen desserts, nuts, caffeine, fried food, salty snack foods, butter, cream cheese, hard cheese, bananas, all exotic fruits and dried fruits, dates, figs, raisins.

Abstain from **ALL FORMS OF SUGAR:** Sucrose, fructose, corn sweeteners, dextrose, maltodextrose, polydextrose, honey, syrups, malt, rice sweeteners.

Abstain from all forms of **SWEETS:** Candies, ice cream, pastries, puddings, donuts, cakes.

Abstain from **ALL FORMS OF FLOUR:** Macaroni, noodles, bread, pizza, crackers, pita bread, bagels, muffins.

Daily Portions

BREAKFAST
1 fruit
1 protein
1 dairy
1 grain

LUNCH
1 protein
1 cup salad or raw
   vegetables
1 vegetable (cooked)

DINNER
1 protein
1 cup salad or raw vegetable
1 vegetable (cooked)
1 starchy vegetable or grain

**4 HOURS
AFTER DINNER**
1 fruit
1 dairy

Serving Sizes

Protein = 4 ounces or 2 eggs
Starchy vegetable and grain = 1 cup
Vegetable = 1 cup
Fruit = 1 cup fresh fruit, ½ cup canned
Dairy = 1 cup (½ cup cottage cheese)
Oil = 1 tablespoon per day
*Spice = 1 teaspoon per day
*Condiments = 1 ounce per day
*Clear broth = 1 cup per day
*Sweeteners = 6 servings per day

(*Caution:* Exclude all sweeteners which contain dextrose, maltodextrose or polydextrose. This includes all of the sweeteners sold in packets.)

Check labels for ingredients. Do not use products which contain sugar, wheat or flour.

- Use decaffeinated coffee, tea and diet soda between meals. Eliminate caffeine because it is an appetite stimulant.
- Use a multivitamin daily.
- Prepare food as follows: bake, broil, grill, boil, steam, stir-fry or panfry in nonstick vegetable sprays.

---

*Optional

Appendix II

Diagnostic Criteria

I had hoped to include information about the newly proposed diagnostic category of Binge Eating Disorder formulated by members of the Eating Disorders Work Group of the DSM-IV Task Force. At this time it seems inconclusive whether the criteria will be included under a separate diagnostic code as "Binge Eating Disorder" or whether it will be included under diagnostic code 307.50 "Eating Disorder Not Otherwise Specified". The diagnostic criteria for binge eating disorder used in field trial according to Spitzer, et al, *International Journal of Eating Disorders*, Volume 11, Number 3, April 1992, page 193 is as follows:

A. Recurrent episodes of binge eating, an episode being characterized by:

    1. Eating, in a discrete period of time (e.g., in any 2-hour period), an amount of food that is definitely larger than most people would eat during a similar period of time.

    2. A sense of lack of control during the episodes, e.g., a feeling that one can't stop eating or control what or how much one is eating.

B. During most binge episodes, at least three of the following behavioral indicators of loss of control:

    1. Eating much more rapidly than usual.

    2. Eating until uncomfortably full.

    3. Eating large amounts of food when not feeling physically hungry.

    4. Eating large amounts of food throughout the day with no planned mealtimes.

    5. Eating alone because of being embarrassed by how much one is eating.

    6. Feeling disgusted with oneself, depressed or feeling very guilty after overeating.

C. Marked distress regarding binge eating.

D. The binge eating occurs, on average, at least twice a week for a 6-month period.

E. Does not currently meet the criteria for bulimia nervosa.

History of weight loss regimens, body image concerns, weight ranges, depressed mood, other substance abuse and identification of the type of foods consumed during a binge which are included in the DSM-III-R diagnostic category 307.51 Bulimia Nervosa are missing in the new category.

Notes

Preface

1. Adelle Davis, **Let's Eat Right to Keep Fit,** Harcourt Brace Jovanovich, New York, 1970, p. 2, reprinted by permission of the publisher.

Chapter One

1. G. Douglas Talbott, M.D., educator and researcher in the field of addictions, is the Director of Impaired Health Professionals Program, Georgia Alcohol and Drug Associates in Smyrna, Georgia. A taped copy of his Keynote Address to the National Eating Disorders Conference is available from U.S. Journal Training, Inc., Enterprise Center, 3201 S.W. 15th Street, Deerfield Beach, FL 33442.

Chapter Two

1. Timothy D. Brewerton, M.D., Margaret M. Heffernan, M.A. and Norman E. Rosenthal, M.D., "Psychiatric Aspects of the Relationship between Eating and Mood," *Nutrition Reviews: Supplement,* May 1986, p. 80.

2. The DSM-III-R Section on Bulimia Nervosa (307.51), pp. 67-69, is reprinted with permission from the **Diagnostic and Statistical Manual of Mental Disorders, Third Edition, Revised,** Washington, DC. Copyright 1987 American Psychiatric Association.

Chapter Three

1. Laurel Mellin, M.A., R.D., Hearing Summary, "Eating Disorders: The Impact on Children and Families," U.S. House of Representatives, Select Committee on Children, Youth and Families, July 31, 1987, San Francisco, CA, p. 1.

2. American Psychiatric Association, **Diagnostic and Statistical Manual of Mental Disorders, Third Edition, Revised,** Washington, DC, American Psychiatric Association, 1987, p. 67.

Chapter Four

1. T. Douglas Talbott, M.D., Keynote Address, "Eating Disorders and Other Addictions: A Holistic Disease," U.S. Journal Training, Inc., Eating Disorders Conference, Atlanta, GA, 1988.

2. Ibid.

3. Ibid.

4. Kenneth Blum, Ph.D., Chief, Division of Alcohol and Substance Abuse, **Some Things You Should Know About Alcoholism,** University of Texas Health Science Center, San Antonio, Texas, Part I.

5. Davis S. Goldbloom, Paul E. Garfinkel and Brian F. Shaw, "Biochemical Aspects of Bulimia Nervosa," *Journal of Psychosomatic Research,* 1991, Vol. 35, Suppl. 1, p. 11.

6. Steven Lally, "Sweet Relief with On-the-Spot Tranquilizers," *Prevention Magazine,* September 1988, Vol. 40, No. 9, p. 30.

7. Ibid.

8. Timothy D. Brewerton, M.D., Margaret M. Heffernan, M.A. and Norman E. Rosenthal, M.D., "Psychiatric Aspects of the Relationship between Eating and Mood," *Nutrition Reviews Supplement,* May 1986, p. 81.

9. Janice Keller Phelps, M.D. and Alan E. Nourse, M.D., **The Hidden Addiction and How to Get Free,** Little Brown, Boston, 1986, p. 76.

10. Bonnie J. Spring, Ph.D., Harris R. Lieberman, Ph.D., Geoffrey Swope and Gail S. Garfield, "Effects of Carbohydrates on Mood and Behavior," *Nutrition Reviews Supplement,* May 1986, p. 52.

11. Talbott, op. cit.

Chapter Five

1. William Dufty, **Sugar Blues,** Warner Books, New York, 1976, p. 22.

2. Robert LeFever, M.D. and Marie Shafe, Ed.D., "Brain Chemistry: Combinations of Foods in the Blood Trigger Effects Very Similar To Alcohol," *Employee Assistance,* March 1991, Vol. 3, No. 8, p. 30.

3. Ibid.

4. Richard J. Wurtman, M.D., "Ways that Foods Can Affect the Brain," *Nutrition Reviews Supplement,* May 1986, p. 3.

5. Robert A. Wallace, **Biology: The World of Life,** Goodyear Publishing, Santa Monica, CA, 1978, p. 267.

6. Anthony Sclafani, "Carbohydrate Taste, Appetite and Obesity, An Overview," *Neuroscience & Biobehavioral Reviews*, 1987, Vol. ll, No. 2, p. 148. Sclafani's paper reviews previous research on sugar appetite and sugar-induced overeating and obesity in the rat, and previews new findings on the rat's taste and appetite for starch and starch-derived polysaccharides.

7. Susan Chollar, "Food for Thought," *Psychology Today*, April 1988, Vol. 22, No. 4, p. 34.

8. Wurtman, op. cit., pp. 3-4.

9. Timothy D. Brewerton, M.D., Margaret M. Heffernan, M.A. and Norman E. Rosenthal, M.D., "Psychiatric Aspects of the Relationship between Eating and Mood," *Nutrition Reviews Supplement*, May 1986, p. 78.

Chapter Six

1. Jules Hirsch, M.D., Chairman, National Institutes of Health Consensus Development Panel, "Health Implications of Obesity," *Annals of Internal Medicine*, 1985, Vol. 103, No. 6, Pt. 2, p. 1074.

2. Willis R. Foster, M.D. and Benjamin T. Burton, Ph.D., "Health Implications of Obesity," *Annals of Internal Medicine*, 1985, Vol. 103, No. 6, Pt. 2, p. 981. The National Institutes of Health organized a consensus development conference to address the health implications of obesity to bring this issue to the attention of physicians, other health professionals and the public, resulting in this report.

3. Joel Killen, Ph.D., Hearing Summary, "Eating Disorders: The Impact on Children and Families," U.S. House of Representatives, Select Committee on Children, Youth and Families Report, July 31, 1987, San Francisco, CA, p. 3.

4. Theodore B. Van Itallie, M.D., "Health Implications of Overweight and Obesity in the United States," *Annals of Internal Medicine,* 1985, Vol. 103, No. 6, Pt. 2, p. 983.

5. George A. Bray, M.D., "Complications of Obesity," *Annals of Internal Medicine,* 1985, Vol. 103, No. 6, Pt. 2, p. 1052.

6. Hirsch, op. cit. p. 1075.

7. Lawrence Garfinkel, "Overweight and Cancer," *Annals of Internal Medicine,* 1985, Vol. 103, No. 6., Pt. 2, p. 1034.

8. Erik P. Eckholm, **The Picture of Health,** W.W. Norton, NY, 1977, p. 78.

9. Bray, op. cit., p. 1054.

10. Ibid, p. 1052.

11. Hirsch, op. cit., p. 1074.

12. Bray, op. cit., p. 1059.

13. Ibid.

14. Garfinkel, op. cit., p. 1034.

15. Robert J. Garrison, M.S. and William P. Castelli, M.D., "Weight and Thirty-year Mortality of Men in the Framingham Study," *Annals of Internal Medicine,* 1985, Vol. 103, No. 6, Pt. 2, p. 1009.

16. Nyda Williams Brown, M.D., "Medical Consequences of Eating Disorders," *Southern Medical Journal,* 1985, Vol. 78, Pt. 4. p. 403.

17. Ibid., p. 404.

18. Hirsch, op. cit., 1074.

19. Frank Webbe, Ph.D., Dean of the School of Psychology, Florida Institute of Technology, Melbourne, Florida in a personal interview reported early findings on suicide attempts from the first 700 respondents to the F.I.T. Food Addiction Research Project.

20. Barbara Schlesier-Stropp, "Bulimia, A Review of the Literature," *American Psychological Association Bulletin,* 1984, Vol. 95, No. 2, p. 251.

21. Ibid., p. 255.

Chapter Seven

1. Janet L. Surrey, Ph.D., "Eating Patterns as a Reflection of Women's Development," Stone Center for Developmental Services and Studies, Wellesley College, Wellesley, Massachusetts, No. 83-06, 1984, p. 2.

2. Rudolph L. Leibel, M.D. and Jules Hirsch, M.D., "Metabolic Characterization of Obesity," *Annals of Internal Medicine,* 1985, Vol. 103, No. 6, Pt. 2, p. 1000.

Chapter Eight

1. Earl Mindell, **Earl Mindell's New and Revised Vitamin Bible,** Warner Communications, New York, 1985, p. 81.

2. Ibid.

3. Adelle Davis, **Let's Eat Right to Keep Fit,** Harcourt Brace Jovanovich, Inc., New York, 1970, pp. 43, 45.

Chapter Ten

1. **Alcoholics Anonymous,** Alcoholics Anonymous World Services, Inc., New York, 1955, p. 124.

Chapter Eleven

1. **Alcoholics Anonymous,** Alcoholics Anonymous World Services, Inc., New York, 1955, pp. 83-84. It is noted that Alcoholics Anonymous World Service Board "feels that this material was written in the general context of the book **(Alcoholics Anonymous)** and was not intended to be separately printed."

Chapter Twelve

1. John M. Kelley, M.A., **Out of the Fog,** Herald House/ Independence Press, Independence, MO, 1992, p. 29.

2. Terence T. Gorski and Merlene Miller, **Staying Sober,** Herald House/Independence Press, Independence, MO, 1986, p. 35.

3. Ibid. p. 67.

4. Ibid. p. 59.

5. Terence T. Gorski, "A Day With Terry Gorski," Blumberg Communications, Orlando, FL, addressing Heritage Food Addiction Alumni Reunion, August 22, 1992.

6. Ibid.

7. **Alcoholics Anonymous,** Alcoholics Anonymous World Services, Inc., New York, 1976, p. 45.

8. Ibid. p. 59.

Bibliography

Alcoholics Anonymous. New York: Alcoholics Anonymous World Services, 1955.

American Psychiatric Association. *Diagnostic and Statistical Manual of Mental Disorders, Third Edition, Revised.* Washington, DC: American Psychiatric Association, 1987.

Blum, Kenneth, Ph.D. **Some Things You Should Know About Alcoholism, Part I.** San Antonio, TX: Division of Alcohol and Substance Abuse, University of Texas Health Science Center.

Bray, George A., M.D. "Complications of Obesity," *Annals of Internal Medicine.* Vol. 103, No. 6, Pt. 2, 1052-1062, 1985.

Brewerton, Timothy D., M.D., Margaret M. Heffernan, M.A. and Norman E. Rosenthal, M.D. "Psychiatric Aspects of the Relationship between Eating and Mood." *Nutrition Reviews: Supplement,* 78-88, May 1986.

Brown, Nyda Williams, M.D. "Medical Consequences of Eating Disorders." *Southern Medical Journal*. Vol. 78, Pt. 4, 403-405, 1985.

Chollar, Susan. "Food For Thought." *Psychology Today*. Vol. 22, No. 4, 30-34, April 1988.

Davis, Adelle. **Let's Eat Right to Keep Fit.** New York: Harcourt Brace Jovanovich, 1970.

Dowling, Lynn. "Food Addiction as Crippling as Alcohol, Drugs: Father Joseph Martin's Story." *The Counselor*. Vol. 5, No. 5, 8-10, Sept./Oct. 1987.

Dufty, William. **Sugar Blues.** New York: Warner Books, 1976.

Eckholm, Erik P. **The Picture of Health.** New York: W.W. Norton & Co., 1977.

Fernstrom, John D., Ph.D. "Acute and Chronic Effects of Protein and Carbohydrate Ingestion and Brain Tryptophan Levels and Serotonin Synthesis." *Nutrition Reviews Supplement*. 25-36, May 1986.

Foster, Willis R., M.D. and Benjamin T. Burton, Ph.D. "Health Implications of Obesity." *Annals of Internal Medicine*. Volume 103, No. 6, Pt. 2, 981-982, 1985.

Garfinkel, Lawrence. "Overweight And Cancer." *Annals of Internal Medicine*. Vol. 103, No. 6, Pt. 2, 1034-1035, 1985.

Garrison, Robert J. M.S. and William P. Catelli, M.D. "Weight and Thirty-year Mortality of Men in the Framingham Study." *Annals Of Internal Medicine*. Vol. 103, No. 6, Pt. 2, 1006-1009, 1985.

Goldbloom, David, Paul E. Garfinkel and Brian F. Shaw. "Biochemical Aspects of Bulimia Nervosa." *Journal of Psychosomatic Research*, Vol. 35, Suppl. 1, 11-22, 1991.

Gorski, Terence T. "A Day with Terry Gorski." Blumberg Communications, Orlando, FL, 1992.

Gorski, Terence T. and Merlene Miller. **Staying Sober.** Independence, MO: Herald House/Independence Press, 1992.

Hirsch, Jules, M.D., Chairman, National Institutes of Health Consensus Development Panel. "Health Implications of Obesity." *Annals Of Internal Medicine.* Vol. 103, No. 6, Pt. 2, 1073-1077, 1985.

Hunter, Beatrice Trum. **The Sugar Trap & How to Avoid It.** Boston: Houghton Mifflin, 1982.

Kelley, John M., M.A. **Out of the Fog.** Independence, MO: Herald House/Independence Press, 1992.

Killen, Joel, Ph.D. Hearing Summary, "Eating Disorders: The Impact on Children and Families." San Francisco: U.S. House of Representatives Select Committee on Children, Youth and Families. 1-3, July 31, 1987.

Lally, Steven. "Sweet Relief with On-the-Spot Tranquilizers." *Prevention Magazine.* Vol. 40, No. 9, 26-133, September 1988.

LeFever, Robert, M.D. and Marie Shafe, Ed.D. "Brain Chemistry, Combinations of Foods in the Blood Trigger Effects Very Similar to Alcohol." *Employee Assistance.* Vol. 3, No. 8, March 1991.

Leibel, Rudolph L., M.D. and Jules Hirsch, M.D. "Metabolic Characterization of Obesity." *Annals of Internal Medicine.* Vol. 103, No. 6, Pt. 2, 1000-1002, 1985.

Mellin, Laurel, M.A., R.D. Hearing Summary, "Eating Disorders: The Impact on Children and Families." San Francisco: U.S. House of Representatives Select Committee on Children, Youth and Families. 1-3, July 31, 1987.

Mindell, Earl. **Earl Mindell's New and Revised Vitamin Bible.** New York: Warner Communications, 1985.

Phelps, Janice Keller, M.D. and Alan E. Nourse, M.D. **The Hidden Addiction and How to Get Free.** Boston: Little, Brown and Company, 1986

Schlesier-Stropp, Barbara. "Bulimia: A Review of the Literature." *American Psychological Association Psychological Bulletin.* Vol. 95, No. 2, 247-257, 1984.

Sclafani, Anthony. "Carbohydrate Taste, Appetite and Obesity: An Overview." *Neuroscience & Biobehavioral Reviews.* Vol. 11 No. 2, 131-153, 1987.

Sheppard, Kay. "Diets: The Problem, Not the Solution." Atlanta, GA: U.S. Journal Training, Inc., Eating Disorders Conference, 1988.

Spring, Bonnie J., Ph.D., Harris R. Lieberman, Ph.D., Geoffrey Swope and Gail S. Garfield. "Effects of Carbohydrates on Mood and Behavior." *Nutrition Reviews Supplement.* 51-59, May 1986.

Surrey, Janet L., Ph.D. "Eating Patterns as a Reflection of Women's Development." No. 83-06. Wellesley, MA: Stone Center for Developmental Services and Studies, Wellesley College, 1984.

Talbott, T. Douglas, M.D. Keynote Address: "Eating Disorders and Other Addictions: A Holistic Disease." Atlanta, GA: U.S. Journal Training, Eating Disorders Conference, 1988.

Van Itallie, Theodore B., M.D. "Health Implications of Overweight and Obesity in the United States." *Annals of Internal Medicine.* Vol. 103, No. 6, Pt. 2, 983-988, 1985.

Wallace, Robert A. **Biology: The World of Life.** Santa Monica, CA: Goodyear Publishing, 1978.

Webbe, Frank, Ph.D. Dean of the School of Psychology, Florida Institute of Technology, interviewed by author, January 18. Melbourne, FL: Florida Institute of Technology, 1989.

Wills-Brandon, Carla. **Eat Like A Lady: Guide For Overcoming Bulimia.** Deerfield Beach, FL: Health Communications, Inc., 1988.

Wills-Brandon, Carla. **Am I Hungry Or Am I Hurting?** San Diego, CA: Recovery Publications, 1993.

Wurtman, Richard J., M.D. "Ways that Foods Can Affect the Brain." *Nutrition Reviews Supplement,* May 1986.

Yudkin, John, M.D. **Sweet and Dangerous.** New York: Peter H. Wyden, 1972.

Professional Care.
Professional Concern.
Professional Counselor . . .
just for you!

Brought to you by Health Communications, Inc., *Professional Counselor* is dedicated to serving the addictions and mental health fields. With Richard Fields, Ph.D., an authority in Dual Diagnosis, serving as editor, and in-depth articles and columns written by and for professionals, you will get the timely information you need to best serve your clients. *Professional Counselor*'s coverage includes:

- Treatment advances
- Mental health and addictions research
- Family, group and special populations therapy
- The latest in counseling techniques
- Listing of upcoming workshops and events
- Managed care and employee assistance programs

Professional Counselor: Serving the Addictions and Mental Health Fields is th magazine for counselors, therapists, addictionologists, psychologists managed-care specialists and employee assistance program personnel.

Order *Professional Counselor* today and take advantage of our specia introductory offer: One year of *Professional Counselor* (6 bimonthy issues) fo just $20.00. That's 23% off the regular subscription price!

Clip and mail to:
Professional Counselor, P.O. Box 607, Mount Morris, IL 61054-7641